Preventing Hazing

Susan Lipkins, Ph.D.

Preventing Hazing

How Parents, Teachers, and Coaches Can Stop the Violence, Harassment, and Humiliation

JOSSEY-BASS
A Wiley Imprint
www.josseybass.com

Published by Jossey-Bass
A Wiley Imprint
989 Market Street, San Francisco, CA 94103-1741   www.josseybass.com

Jossey-Bass books and products are available through most bookstores. To contact Jossey-Bass directly call our Customer Care Department within the U.S. at 800-956-7739, outside the U.S. at 317-572-3986, or fax 317-572-4002.

Jossey-Bass also publishes its books in a variety of electronic formats. Some content that appears in print may not be available in electronic books.

Library of Congress Cataloging-in-Publication Data

Lipkins, Susan, date.
    Preventing hazing : how parents, teachers, and coaches can stop the violence, harassment, and humiliation / Susan Lipkins.
        p. cm.
    Includes bibliographical references and index.
    ISBN-13: 978-0-7879-8178-5 (pbk.)
    ISBN-10: 0-7879-8178-8 (pbk.)
    1. Bullying in schools—Prevention.   2. Hazing—Prevention.   I. Title.
    LB3013.3.L56 2006
    371.5'8—dc22   2006012333

Printed in the United States of America
FIRST EDITION
PB Printing   10 9 8 7 6 5 4 3 2 1

Contents

*This book is dedicated to the courageous individuals
who have broken the code of silence.*

Acknowledgments

I am fortunate to have a core of special people who supported me throughout the year in which I wrote this book. The initial inspiration came from a close friend and colleague, Stephanie Daniels, who had the insight to recognize that the theories I had developed about hazing needed to be published. Stephanie and her husband, Mark Smith, worked with me as we filmed the families who were traumatized by hazing. Their hard work and deeply felt conversations have been an integral part of my interviews and ideas. Luckily, Dr. Roger Pierangelo, a longtime friend and a brilliant author, connected me to the right publisher. Roger has been available at all hours of the day and night, to support, guide, and help me through this incredibly exciting project. Karen Savoy, a unique and powerful individual, opened her heart and soul and helped me enter into the closely knit circle of those who have been affected by hazings. Hank Nuwer, author and well-known expert on hazing, has educated me—about hazing, media, and publishing.

The true experts, however, are those who weathered the difficult times. I am deeply appreciative of all the students, parents, coaches, lawyers, and others who shared their intimate stories, including Pat, Carol, Eleanor, Beverly, Kevin, Jerry, and Jake, as well as the many, many brave people who helped me learn about the psychology of hazing.

Thanks to those who assisted me in a variety of ways, including those who let me use their photos on the cover, such as Halle Ornstein and Steve Interdonati. Thanks to those friends who gave me hope and energy, such as Darren Campo and Lisa Dubin. Thanks to Alan Rinzler for green-lighting the project and for having faith that I could actually write this book. I would like to acknowledge and thank Seth Schwartz, my editor, for his time and friendship. He was always available, always energetic, always knowledgeable, and always able to guide me, gently, through the birth of this book.

As I write these acknowledgments, I am realizing how much emotion, time, and energy I have spent creating this book. I would not have had the confidence to pitch the idea nor the strength to write the book without the unyielding support of Barbara Deutsch. There are so many others who were kind enough to critique my writing, add their stories, do the surveys, and in myriad ways support me as I wrote this book. Thanks to all of you.

My family, Zachary, Julia, and Jack, were troopers, as they tolerated my relentless conversations about hazing. Working through the painful stories and being pulled emotionally by the events and experiences of those who have been hazed has had profound effects on my family and on me. It is difficult to properly acknowledge all those close to me, for the significant amount of time, words, opinions, and help that they gave to me. Most especially, however, is the gratitude and appreciation that I have for my insightful and supportive husband, Jack, who fed me, both figuratively and literally, as I wrote this book. Throughout many long days and nights, he provided me with an unending amount of patience and understanding, indulging my passion to write and tell these stories. I am truly grateful for Jack's enthusiasm, pride, and steadfast support. I deeply cherish him and I am lucky to have his respect and love.

Preventing Hazing

Introduction

It was September 2003, and a story broke about a hazardous hazing in Bellmore, New York. Three freshman football players for Mepham High School were brutally beaten and sexually molested by their teammates during a preseason football camp. This hazing occurred in a school district that is about twenty minutes away from my home and office. As I read and reread the news reports, I wondered why students would beat and sodomize their fellow teammates. As a psychologist who has spent the last twenty years treating children and adolescents, I felt that if *I* didn't know why these behaviors occurred, who did?

With each new detail reported by the local and national news agencies, I became more committed to investigating and understanding hazing. I began to research the topic, only to discover that there was a very small body of information on why people haze. How could this be? My early training as an anthropologist led me to collect raw data by interviewing students, parents, and coaches who had been involved in hazing. As I listened, I started to see patterns in their stories. I conducted research through additional surveys and interviews and spoke with a variety of professionals who were involved in hazing prevention. My efforts led to answers about why hazing occurs, how hazing skids out of control and becomes dangerous, what we can do to help those involved, and how to prevent it in the first place.

My intention is to have this book revolutionize how hazing is perceived and to develop and implement programs to prevent hazing. I hope to inspire individuals and communities to become agents of change. I know this won't be an easy task. Hazing has occurred throughout history and is now firmly embedded in our culture.

HAZING THROUGH THE AGES

The hazing that we see today has roots in the various *rites of passage* that have occurred for centuries. Rites of passage are a set of events that groups require to mark a change in an individual's status. All civilizations celebrate certain developmental changes, such as birth, death, and marriage. The specific celebrations or traditions are a reflection of the values of that society.

Every culture has a unique way to mark these rites of passage. Each step of the tradition is carefully orchestrated, and each time the pattern is repeated exactly. These rituals are led by authority figures, who have special status, knowledge, or power within the group. The sequence of the ritual, the pomp and circumstance, and, most important, the leader of the group, ensure that the ritual is being carried out in the way prescribed by previous generations.

One of the rites of passage that is still celebrated today is the welcoming of an adolescent into adulthood. In tribes such as the Ambonwari of Papau, New Guinea, the rite of passage, and the celebration, have not changed for thousands of years.[1] Many Christian religions have confirmations to mark this transformation—a change from child to adult, with more power and responsibility. Similarly, Jewish males at age thirteen are required to complete a bar mitzvah, which includes learning a prescribed set of prayers that must be said in Hebrew. In each example, the rite is led by a select member or members of the group—a *wasamari* (a "father's father" who protects an adolescent boy during the initiation ritual) for the Ambonwari tribe, a bishop or priest for the confirmation, and a rabbi for a bar mitzvah. The actual prayers and requirements of these rites have not changed for centuries. The meaning and the symbolism remain, even if the celebration that occurs afterward has changed over time. The specifics of the celebration reflect the values of the young adult's family and culture.

Hazing is also part of the rites of passage for many groups. The hazing is the activity that concretizes the passage of the individual's status, from a person outside the group to one accepted into the group, or from someone with low status to someone with higher status.

However, unlike most traditional rites of passage, the hazing that is currently practiced by middle, high school, and college students is not authorized, not controlled. The symbolism of the original ceremony is often lost. The leaders, themselves, are unrestrained. The hazing does not demonstrate skills that are necessary for the group's cultural survival, nor does it serve any other positive function. In fact, the physical and emotional pain that hazing inflicts is the only outcome, and it is misconstrued by the participants as proof of their strength or mental fortitude.

Hazing has been recorded as part of history for centuries. Rituals in Ancient Greece and Rome included educating boys in ways that are reminiscent of hazing. For example, there were special mentoring relationships that required servitude, kidnapping, and sexual favors.[2] Hazing new students seemed to be an expected practice among students in European universities during the Middle Ages as well. Newcomers drank concoctions that included urine. They endured tortures such as scraping skin off their ears.[3] In the sixteenth century, Martin Luther supported hazing, claiming that it strengthened the student and prepared him for the obstacles of adulthood. During nineteenth-century England, Dr. Christopher Wordsworth (nephew of the poet William Wordsworth) is credited with legalizing *fagging* (meaning toiling, working hard). Fagging includes beatings, humiliation, and servitude, among other hazing-like practices.[4] Fagging was encouraged by the school's administration, believing that it was a good way to teach obedience.

HAZING IN THE UNITED STATES

Hazing has been reported in the United States since the 1600s, when Oxford University students came to Harvard and introduced fagging and other hazing activities. In the 1700s, student hazing was an accepted part of Harvard life. In fact, the sophomore classes actually published the hazing customs and gave them to incoming freshmen. The new students had to wear special clothes, run personal errands, and bring sports equipment for the older students. Hazing at Harvard fraternities and clubs began in 1781 when Phi Beta Kappa was organized and continued in 1795 with the creation of the Hasty Pudding Club. Hazing traditions and activities were part of these and other organizations, and stories about their "pranks" continued into the 1800s. In 1818, the Medical Faculty Society, a secret organization, was created by students to wreak havoc on Harvard's campus. The society's initiation rites made new members risk expulsion by issuing fake degrees, painting university statues, and ridiculing their professors and school administrators.[5]

Hazing spread to other colleges and universities throughout the United States. Pranks, harmful actions, and dangerous initiations were known to occur between upperclassmen and underclassmen and among other groups at Amherst College, Cornell University, and the University of Michigan. Reports of hazing in the early part of the twentieth century are part of the history of many colleges, including Franklin and Marshall, Indiana University, and the University of Texas. Throughout the remainder of the twentieth century, hazing activities continued to flourish. Paddling, extreme calisthenics, sleep deprivation, scavenger hunts, kidnapping, branding, drowning, and the consumption of huge amounts of alcohol became more prevalent.

Hazing in the twenty-first century employs many of the initiation rites and rituals that have been used for centuries. However, it seems that today's hazings are more frequent, more demeaning, more violent, and much more sexual. We are also finding evidence that students are beginning to be hazed in middle school. In addition, the stereotypical notion that hazing happens only to boys who are involved in aggressive sports is not true. We find that girls and boys are just as likely to be hazed and that hazing occurs in nonaggressive activities such as band, debate, cheerleading, and even church groups! Here are some examples:

- In September 2002, Kristin High and Kenitha Saafir, students at California State University, Los Angeles, drowned during an alleged Alpha Kappa Alpha pledge activity. They were blindfolded, had their hands tied together, and were led into the Pacific Ocean at night.

- In July 2004, an initiation into the band at a Georgia high school included "buying" freshmen, who were then collared and led around on a leash. The boys were dressed as girls, in outfits that included pantyhose, thongs, and tiaras, and paraded in school in front of students and faculty.

- In the fall of 2004, at a parochial boarding school for girls in New Hampshire, seniors required the freshmen to simulate oral sex with bananas and answer sexually explicit questions. Here, as in other schools, just being a freshman was a reason to be hazed.

- In September 2004, Gordie Bailey, a freshman at the University of Colorado, Boulder, died due to alcohol overdose that was part of a fraternity pledge activity.

- In December 2004, freshmen girls on a debate team in a Texas high school were required to move fifty-pound debate tubs and team luggage several times on a trip, and they were humiliated by the debate team's student officers.

These examples are just the tip of the iceberg. Although obtaining the exact number of hazings that occur each year is almost impossible, we can get a picture of the current state of affairs from a study conducted by Alfred University in 1999. This study was the first major, large-scale attempt to quantify and explain hazing in the United States. The study found that hazing occurs frequently in both high school and college. Overall, one in five students will be hazed, with girls and boys equally likely to be victims of hazing. In addition, the Alfred study found the following:

- Hazing often starts at a young age. Twenty-five percent of students reported first being hazed before age thirteen.

- Hazing occurs frequently among high school students. Forty-eight percent of students involved in a group activity reported being hazed, and thirty percent reported performing illegal activities as part of their initiation. Even "safe groups" are not immune to hazing. Twenty-four percent of students involved in church groups have been hazed.

- More than a quarter of a million students experienced some form of hazing in order to join a college athletic team. Sixty-six percent were subjected to humiliating hazing, such as being yelled or sworn at; being forced to wear embarrassing clothing; or being forced to deprive themselves of sleep, food, or personal hygiene. Fifty percent were required to participate in drinking contests or alcohol-related hazing, and twenty percent were subjected to unacceptable and potentially illegal hazing. They were kidnapped, beaten, or tied up and abandoned. They were also forced to commit crimes: stealing or

destroying property, making crank phone calls, or
harassing others.

As shocking as these facts are, all statistics underestimate the
amount of hazing activities that students actually engage in. Hazing usually goes unreported and, when hazardous, is underreported.
Students often feel as though they have no one safe to turn to, no
one who is trained to deal with their psychological wounds, and
no one to actually report the crime to. Their perceptions are correct. Currently, there are no government agencies that accept
reports of hazing, such as exists for child abuse, and no agencies that
provide counseling and protection services, such as exists for victims of domestic violence or rape. In addition, there are no official
programs that track hazing and no funding source that provides for
ongoing research about why hazing occurs and how we can prevent
it. It's my hope that this book will spur a movement to rectify this
situation.

HOW TO USE THIS BOOK

Preventing Hazing is the first book to offer methods and techniques
to help parents, teachers, and coaches prevent hazing. These methods and techniques are rooted in child development theory, educational best practices, and years of psychological and educational
research. It can be used by everyone. The book explains the dynamics of hazing, how and why it happens. It offers real-life solutions to
help prevent hazing in the future.

Chapter One begins by defining *hazing* and *hazardous hazing*. It
also explains how and why hazing occurs.

Chapter Two details methods and techniques that parents,
teachers, and coaches can use to prevent hazing in their communities. Specific, practical hazing information will educate both adults
and students.

Chapter Three discusses early warning signs that will help parents, teachers, and coaches recognize the symptoms of hazing. Questions to ask your child about their possible involvement in hazing are provided.

Chapter Four explains what to do if a child has been the victim of a hazing. All aspects of crisis intervention are explored, including how to deal with medical and psychological issues. Techniques for talking with a child involved in a hazing are provided, as are details on how and when to report an incident, as well as potential legal remedies.

Chapter Five deals with the perpetrator. As you'll discover, all too often "good kids" who were once victims eventually become perpetrators. The psychological and legal ramifications of this are discussed, and concrete interventions are recommended.

Chapter Six is very important because it lays the groundwork for promoting true changes in our culture. This section examines the power and responsibility of the bystander. Concrete methods to empower the bystander, as an individual, and to organize bystanders, as a group, are described.

Chapter Seven explains how communities can heal themselves after a hazing. It also provides pragmatic interventions and solutions for the future.

Preventing Hazing includes the true stories (some names have been changed to protect their identities) of students who have experienced hazing in high schools and colleges. You will hear from students, parents, and coaches, as well as others who have been involved in hazing. Their pain, their wisdom, and their advice are integrated into each chapter. The book concludes with a Resource Guide, including books, Web sites, and films, which parents, teachers, coaches, and students can use to learn more about hazing.

You may find the material in this book shocking, because you may not have realized that hazing is embedded in our society and that it is likely to touch your child, either directly or indirectly. However, with your help, hazing is something that *can be changed.*

Since I began studying this topic, the incidences of hazing that have been reported have increased tremendously. Each time victims read a report, they are given strength to come forward and expose the hazing that they have endured. Little by little, we are supporting those who break the code of silence, those who are brave enough to stand up and change society. I hope you will join the cause.

Understanding Hazing

In late August 2003, in Preston Township, Pennsylvania, sixty-eight teenage boys, aged thirteen to eighteen, from Mepham High School in Bellmore, New York, participated in a preseason football camp. Five coaches supervised the intense football drills. During breaks, the kids retreated to their cabins, where some of the freshmen, barely weighing more than a hundred pounds, were being tortured by the varsity team members, all weighing in at over two hundred pounds. Three boys were beaten with large plastic garbage bags filled with chunks of ice. The brutality was evidenced by welts and black and blue marks all over the face, chest, arms, and legs of the freshmen. At other times, the boys were sodomized with broomsticks, golf balls, and pine cones covered in mineral ice to increase the pain. These physical and sexual assaults continued day and night, in the bunks and by the lake, for five days. The hazing was not reported until three weeks later, when two boys were bleeding from their rectums and sought medical attention.

This story was too scary to be true. That's how I felt when the news broke in Long Island, New York, in mid-September 2003. As a psychologist specializing in adolescents, I couldn't understand how or why such brutality could occur. I couldn't stop thinking about the scenes that were being reported on a daily basis. To this day, the stories from that football camp still shock me.

It is surprising to learn that hazing is an everyday occurrence throughout the country and the world. As I realized this, I began to understand the magnitude of the issue, and I believe that there must be reasons why this behavior has existed from biblical days until now. This chapter explores the dimensions of hazing: how it happens, with whom it happens, when it happens, and why it happens.

WHAT IS HAZING?

Hazing is a buzzword that has many meanings, all of which seem to change according to who is using it and in what context. For example, the National Panhellenic Conference, which represents college sororities, does not like to use the words *pledging* or *hazing;* they prefer *new member education*. Athletic coaches usually use the word *tradition*. For those who have participated in some kind of initiation rite, hazing may refer to the exciting or memorable part of that experience. For those who have never participated, it may mean something they have read or heard about.

In 1999, Alfred University in Alfred, New York, conducted a survey on hazing. It is the only substantial published study and is considered the "gold standard" of hazing research.[1] For the purposes of their survey, they used the following definition of hazing:

> Any activity expected of someone joining a group that humiliates, degrades, abuses or endangers, regardless of the person's willingness to participate. This does not include activities such as rookies carrying the balls, team parties with community games, or going out with your teammates, unless an atmosphere of humiliation, degradation, abuse or danger arises.

Another helpful definition comes from Mothers Against School Hazing (MASH).[2]

They define hazing as follows:

> A broad term encompassing any action or activity which does not contribute to the positive development of a person; which inflicts or intends to cause physical or mental harm or anxieties; which may demean, degrade, or disgrace any person, regardless of location, intent or consent of participants, or any action or situation, which intentionally or unintentionally endangers a student for admission into or affiliation with any student organization.

My definition piggybacks on those definitions, but it's more specific in terms of who, what, where, and why. It's important to understand that hazing has characteristics that are very different from other kinds of violence that occur among teens and adults.

I believe that hazing is a process based on a tradition that is used by groups to maintain a hierarchy (a "pecking order") within the group. Regardless of consent, the rituals require individuals to engage in activities that are physically and psychologically stressful. These activities can be exhausting, humiliating, degrading, demeaning, and intimidating. They result in significant physical and emotional discomfort. More specifically, hazing

- Involves a repetition of a tradition

- Is a process

- Maintains a hierarchy within a group

- Intends to create closeness in a group

- Involves psychological and physical stress

Let's take a closer look at each of these characteristics.

Hazing Repeats a Tradition

Tradition is the most distinguishing factor of a hazing as compared with other kinds of group behaviors. These traditions may have significance and relevance to the group, or they may have had a specific meaning that has been lost over time. Traditions are the cornerstone of most hazing, and they've usually been passed down from previous generations of the group.

Traditions may involve physical activities that are symbolic (such as lighting candles at a sorority event) or challenging (such as doing strenuous calisthenics). Likewise traditions may involve psychological elements, such as causing humiliation (having boys wear girls' undergarments in public, for example), which are usually more powerful than the physical ones. Other common hazing traditions involve eating extremely spicy foods, shaving hair, and acting as servants.

Hazing Involves a Process

From my point of view, hazing is a process. There is a beginning, a middle, and an end. Hazing involves planning that often takes weeks or months to prepare and carry out. First, a person is invited or expected to participate in a group activity. Once the person shows interest, the *test* part occurs, and those in charge believe that it's their right and duty to make sure that this person is worthy of being a member of their group. To do this, a sequence of activities is required.

Hazings that occur as part of fraternities and sororities are repetitions of traditions and initiation rites that involve a long process. Weeks before the *pledges* arrive, the members of the fraternity or sorority are planning where and when the pledge activities will occur. The person responsible for organizing this is called the *pledge master*. Frequently, the entire group of active members participates in the actual events, such as requiring pledges to drink large amounts of alcohol in a specific time frame or to memorize huge amounts of trivia about the fraternity or the sorority. In some colleges, the initiation process occurs over the course of four weeks, whereas in others, it occurs over the course of an entire semester. The kinds of pledge activities change as the process continues and then culminates in a *hell week*, which encompasses the most severe physical and psychological part of the hazing. At the end, there is an initiation ceremony: the pledges are now accepted and become members of the sorority or fraternity.

Hazing Maintains a Hierarchy

Hazing is used by groups to create and maintain a specific social structure and hierarchy. The hierarchy, which has already been established, is a significant part of the group dynamics. The newcomer, sometimes called the *newbie*, "needs" to understand the hierarchy, and it's up to the senior members of the group to enforce it. In the military, fraternities, and sororities, the concept of *respect* is considered significant. They want the newbies to respect their "elders," those members who are already part of the established group. In athletics, the concept of hierarchy is similar, where seniors and varsity members hold dominance over freshmen and junior varsity players.

Essentially, hazing necessitates unequal status. Those who are new have less power than those who have been part of the group for a longer time. Whether we want to admit it or not, this drive to maintain the status quo and established hierarchy is seen in almost every example of group behavior. The new kid on the block, the new teacher in the school, or the new cheerleader are all treated with less respect than those who have been established, whose credentials have been verified, and who have already proven themselves "acceptable" to the group. Upon completion of the initiation process, the newcomer is transformed from a newbie, with no rights and privileges, to a member with a higher status.

Hazing Intends to Create Closeness

Members of sports teams, fraternities, clubs, and other organizations that require an initiation rite believe that the group will grow closer by sharing an experience. In truth, those on the same level, such as pledges in a fraternity or freshmen on a hockey team, may feel close to one another as they will have shared the same initiation. However, these same people won't feel trusting or positive toward those who actually hazed them. Instead the newbies often feel anger and frustration. Such negative feelings could either be conscious or unconscious, and they're usually not discussed with the leaders or senior members of the group. It's probable though that the group of hazers will feel closer once they have hazed, because now they're "partners in crime" and will need to protect themselves should something serious occur.

Groups that haze have no doubt that it is a necessary experience that ensures bonding. To combat this, some hazing experts have suggested substituting positive bonding activities, such as ski trips, rock climbing, or kayaking. What has happened though is that now the groups, such as fraternities and sororities, do the rock climbing or other positive bonding activity suggested by the Nationals (the national office of the fraternity or sorority), *as well as* the usual local traditions—including hazing—that are not sanctioned by the national organization. In fact, a study reported in the *American Journal of Health Behavior* in 2005 found that those involved in hazing were also more likely to be involved in team-building activities. This seems to support my belief that providing positive team-building experiences doesn't replace hazing traditions.

Hazing Involves Stress

Being able to cope with stress seems to be an attribute that's emphasized by all kinds of groups. Those seeking acceptance are often "stressed out" on purpose, in order to measure their ability to cope. For example, in high schools, freshmen athletes are often required to do more conditioning activities than everyone else, and they're treated more harshly if they're late for practice. It's also common for freshmen to carry the heavy equipment before and after practice and games, set up the equipment, and shower after all the senior team members have finished.

An Insider's View of Hazing

I think the most important thing for people to know about hazing is that it doesn't bring people together. What it really does is to slowly break a person down mentally, so they relinquish control to their hazers. Pledging changes a person if they relinquish control. The brothers say you aren't a man or aren't worthy of being a member if you don't eat or drink some disgusting mixture. For example, I had to eat whole onions, unpeeled, drink a gallon of milk as fast as possible, and finish an entire keg of beer between ten pledges. A keg is over two hundred beers, and we did it in forty-three minutes, with a lot of vomiting so we would not get alcohol poisoning. Hell week was worse. Each night, we had to go to the fraternity house, clean it, then go into the cold, dank, smelly basement, blindfold ourselves, and recite passages from a book. All of this was done to strike fear into us and mess with our heads so we followed without hesitation, even though the brothers said it was to make us closer.

As I was being hazed, I was never afraid, I was angry the whole time. I hated my pledge brothers because they were getting brainwashed and wanted to do everything they were told. I hated the people who were hazing me too. I look at them as cowards because of the way they spoke to me, the things they yelled at me, they never would have said if they weren't in that position of authority.

—STEVE, freshman pledge in a National fraternity

In college, Greek life pledges know that they may be dedicating anywhere from a few weeks to an entire semester fulfilling the requirements of the fraternity or sorority. The pledge masters are strict, and fines are given if a pledge doesn't fulfill the required pledge activity. Often pledges are sleep deprived, exposed to the elements (such as being outside during cold winter months without anything other than underwear), and assaulted. (They still get paddled or hit, often with brutal force.) Because they have to maintain a specific academic average, all the while being sleep deprived, being involved in a myriad of questionable activities, and having the pressure to conform, pledges suffer significant psychological stress.

A WORD ON BULLYING

The terms *hazing* and *bullying* are often used interchangeably. Though both are aggressive acts sometimes committed by high school and college students, they are very different. Some educators and professionals are tempted to lump them together and use the same preventive strategies for both. In my opinion, however, because they are different, appropriate interventions are needed for each.

Bullying is an intentional act of aggression that is meant to harm a victim either physically, psychologically, or both. Bullies usually operate alone or in small groups and choose to victimize individuals whom they perceive as vulnerable. Victims attract bullies by their smaller stature, their younger age, or their lower social status. Frequently, there is only one specific victim, who is often a scapegoat. There are no traditions involved in bullying, nor are there authority figures or leaders.

Bullies usually want something—maybe money, maybe a student's lunch, maybe homework answers, or maybe just attention. Bullies may also act simply to demonstrate that they are more powerful, thereby ensuring their status as "tough guys." Often peers of a bully are intimidated and therefore appear to "respect" the bully but are really just in fear of him.

In contrast, hazing involves a large enough group where some participants are hazers, some are watchers, and some are hazed. The hazed members are part of an identified group, such as freshmen on a soccer team. Hazers are acting on the behalf of a group and usually have no intent to harm or to gain individual status or objects from those that are hazed. Those that haze are passing on a tradition and maintaining a hierarchy.

Both bullying and hazing have been increasing in frequency and severity over the past ten years, and both require the attention of parents, teachers, school administrators, and communities. For a further discussion of bullies, read Barbara Coloroso's excellent book, *The Bully, the Bullied, and the Bystander*.

WHAT IS HAZARDOUS HAZING?

Hazing occurs on a continuum from mild to severe. In its mildest forms, hazing involves such things as requiring new group members to address older group members with respectful terms such as *Sir* and *Ma'am* or requiring fraternity or sorority pledges to dress up on certain days. On athletic teams, the freshmen might have to get water for the older members.

Hazardous hazing occurs when traditions or initiation rites skid out of control and cause *significant* and *lasting* physical or psychological damage. When hazardous hazing occurs, everyone in the group, including the perpetrators (those who have planned and carried out the actions), the bystanders (those who have watched and not actively participated), and the victims (those who have received the hazing), may be psychologically traumatized. The families of those involved, the coaches, and the other supervisors may also be traumatized even if they weren't present during the hazardous hazing. Their trauma may be evident immediately, or it may be delayed for months or years or even decades. More specifically, hazardous hazing

- Involves a repetition of dangerous traditions

- Occurs when those in charge have lost control and judgment

- Intends to create closeness in the group but that closeness is undermined

- Involves a plan without an assessment of danger

- Can lead to serious physical or psychological damage

It's important to understand these characteristics in order to comprehend the true nature of hazardous hazing. Let's take a more in-depth look at them.

Hazardous Hazing Repeats Dangerous Traditions

Oftentimes people who have been involved in a hazing don't see the danger in the process. For example, in a high school class that I visited, one junior described how he locked a teammate in a locker. The victim was sitting next to him and laughed about it. Simultaneously, a girl sitting close by turned pale as she imagined being stuck in the locker and having a panic attack, because she is claustrophobic. Even activities that appear benign to some people have the potential of turning into a hazardous hazing.

Hazardous hazing traditions often involve a combination of these, and other, dangerous acts:

- *Physical assault:* including paddling, beating, punching, burning, or branding

- *Unlawful restraint:* including taping someone to a bench, tree, or goalpost

- *Confinement:* including in car trunks, lockers, closets, or basements

- *Ingesting substances:* including excessive amounts of foods or combinations of nonfood substances

- *Alcohol consumption:* such as requiring dangerous amounts of drinking or combinations of alcohol to be consumed, sometimes within a short time frame

- *Sexual activities:* such as simulating sexual acts, performing sodomy, or being involved in forced sexual events or rape

- *Kidnapping:* such as blindfolding and disorienting students before leaving them far from home or campus

- *Exposure:* to extreme temperature and weather conditions, sometimes causing hypothermia or heat exhaustion

- *Humiliation:* involving inappropriate and demeaning acts, such as using a permanent magic marker to circle fat on sorority girls or doing the "elephant walk" (The elephant walk requires students to be nude and walk in a circle, with one thumb in their mouth and the other in the anus of the person in front of them. On command, the leader demands that they switch thumbs.)

- *Physical degradation:* such as being doused or pelted with urine, feces, rotten eggs, and other assorted garbage

- *Psychological degradation:* such as treating the victim like a servant or slave

- *Physical stress and exhaustion:* requiring extreme physical exertion or extreme deprivation of sleep, food, water, showers, or the freedom to speak

- *Dangerous situations:* being exposed to potentially life-threatening situations, such as being drunk and blind-folded while crossing ravines or walking into the ocean

There are other kinds of hazing that are not outlined here but that meet these criteria.

These kinds of hazing leave psychological scars that are even deeper than those that require medical intervention. The victims feel violated and helpless. If they want to remain in the group, they must repress their thoughts about these experiences and deny their hurt and negative feelings. Those who come forth feel betrayed and may face a *second hazing,* in which the group's members harass the individual for reporting the incident. (There's more discussion on the second hazing in Chapter Seven.)

Hazardous Hazing Lacks Control and Judgment

Hazardous hazing occurs when there is no one truly in control and no one who is able to make appropriate judgments about the situation. When hazing skids out of bounds, the group leaders have failed to create safety controls. Those leaders include the immediate authority figure, such as the pledge master or the team captain, as well as all the supervisors and administrators who are above them.

In many cases, the group leaders are probably not even focused on the possible consequences; they are simply caught up in the intensity of the moment or repetition of a tradition. The group leaders may lose control because they are drunk or stoned or their emotional state is inflamed. This often occurs to young adults (ages fourteen to twenty-four), who have the feeling that they are invulnerable and invincible. They are denying reality, falsely believing that they are in control of the situation. The leaders above them—the coaches, fraternity presidents, principals, or superintendents—have not provided safe environments. They have failed to teach the groups how to create safety nets, how to determine dangerous situations, and how to prevent hazardous hazing. They have also failed to teach the groups why safety nets are necessary for the group's survival and well-being.

How are administrators supposed to control students who are not compliant? Perhaps the analogy to drunk driving is applicable. After many years, and many laws, drunk-driving fatalities have been reduced. High school students actually plan parties and choose a designated driver. Friends often actually take keys away from others who are too intoxicated to drive. As the saying goes, "Friends don't let friends drive drunk." The education and public service announcements have worked. And remember that this is the same population, in terms of age and psychological stage, as those who are involved in hazing.

Hazardous Hazing Undermines Groups

The intention of hazing is to develop closeness among a group of people. After hazing skids into the hazardous zone, the group may experience a tightening. This, however, is something like "batten down the hatches and make sure no one tells about what happened." The closeness is out of fear of being discovered, not out of friendship, respect, or true camaraderie. The bonding that occurs under these circumstances is questionable and probably uncomfortable to most members of the group. The participants who have a strong moral compass will experience the most anxiety and discomfort.

Participating in a hazardous hazing may have the opposite effect of the one originally intended by the leaders. Such an experience may teach an individual *not to trust* because they realize how a situation can turn deadly.

Hazardous Hazing Involves Dangerous Plans

Hazardous hazing occurs when those organizing the event don't perceive the inherent dangers in their plan. Usually, the group leaders believe that their plan is no more dangerous than the one that they were subjected to. This may or may not be true. The fact that others have survived a similar hazing doesn't mean that the original concept was not dangerous to begin with. It means that they were lucky. Therefore the original plan or tradition needs to be assessed for its safety, no matter how many times it has been accomplished without mishaps.

Hazing may be tweaked in order to "outdo" those that were done in the past, or in order to add some originality. This is very common and may be one of the factors that lead hazing into the hazardous zone. Adding just a bit more alcohol, or water, or calisthenics, or freezing conditions, may be just the amount needed to create lethal situations.

In addition, no one truly knows how much his body, or someone else's, can tolerate before organs fail or hypothermia sets in. Perhaps the most dangerous part of these plans is that there is no one on "emergency duty." There is no one trained and no one alert enough to make the call that the situation is spinning out of control. It is as though the "designated driver" is missing.

Hazardous Hazing Leads to Serious Physical and Psychological Issues

Hazardous hazing often results in a long, complicated array of physical and emotional problems. Alcohol poisoning and drug overdose are common with high school and college students. But the difference in the case of hazardous hazing is that those who are being coerced, either directly or via implied peer pressure, are forced to exceed the amount that they would willingly consume under typical circumstances. Neither the newbie nor the group leader knows how much will be too much for each individual.

The consequences of alcohol and drug overdoses range from an intense hangover to situations that require medical treatments. Some victims need to have their stomachs pumped; some require CPR; and, some die. Other medical conditions resulting from alcohol and drug-related hazardous hazing events include broken bones and fractures caused by car accidents and fights.

Burning of the skin or of internal mucous linings, such as the mouth, esophagus, and stomach may also occur due to contact with fire, or with large amounts of spicy substances. Sometimes jalapenos and other kinds of hot spices are added to alcohol in order to make people vomit, which allows them to continue to consume more drinks. A scary example of this can be seen in the following story.

In a college in Georgia, the fraternity pledge process began with the consumption of an extreme quantity of chopped raw onions. (This is a common theme, to begin the process by eating things that are very spicy, and in fact, sometimes hot sauce, curry, and other kinds of spices are added to increase the intensity of the experience.) For some pledges, the onions burned third-degree holes in the lining of their mouths. The burns were not limited to the mouth and continued to cause inflammation and damage to the pledges' esophagus and digestive tract. Many pledges suffered from significant stomachaches and painful diarrhea, and subsequent hemorrhoids and rectal bleeding. Some pledges were so affected that they were not even able to talk, drink, or eat for several days. They risked becoming dehydrated and missed several days of classes.

Even more disturbing than physical pain are the various sexual activities that may be required either by force or by peer pressure. Sodomy among males is not uncommon and includes putting fingers, objects, or in the worst cases, broomsticks, pine cones, and golf balls covered in Icy Hot into the rectums of the victims. The physical repercussions have ranged from the mild ones to those requiring repetitive rectal surgery. Some sororities have even encouraged pledges to meet the needs of frat brothers, which may include intercourse or oral sex and at its worst becomes date rape.

The psychological aftermath of hazardous hazing can be even more traumatic than the physical. In my interviews of those who have been involved in severe physical hazing events, the victims all state that their wounds heal but not their souls. The psychic damage is probably impossible to measure. It haunts the individual for life.

Victims who come forward and report an incident can be harassed by the group or the group leaders. The isolation, degradation, and humiliation can become so intense that severe psychological problems arise. Many victims are actually physically threatened and intimidated. High school students sometimes switch schools or their family moves away. In every case that I investigated, when college students broke the *code of silence*, they were so harassed and threatened that they felt they had no choice but to transfer to another school.

In the immediate aftermath of a hazardous hazing, such as one that has led to a severe injury or death, all those involved, directly or indirectly, are often in a state of shock. They're not able to concentrate and are often hysterical and extremely anxious. These conditions may fade, only to be replaced by other psychological conditions that continue over time and interfere with general functioning. Emotions can be overwhelming, marked by crying, phobias, paranoia, anxiety, and depression. (There's a complete discussion of the psychological traumas in Chapters Four, Five and Six.)

WHO'S INVOLVED IN HAZING?

At this point, you're probably wondering who would be involved in such absurd, cruel, and dangerous activities. It couldn't possibly be anyone you know. The truth is that anyone and everyone may be involved in hazing! There is no one profile of students who are victimized by hazing or students who are hazers.

Perpetrators

Hazing begins with the people who are leaders and have control of the group. They're the *perpetrators*. They're usually the senior members of the group or those who have significant status due to their size, status, abilities, or personality.

Some perpetrators have been bullies or troublemakers and have a history of out-of-control, aggressive behaviors. However, it's important to understand that *most* perpetrators don't have such a history. Many are star athletes, honor students, or student council members. Most perpetrators are made, not born. They are made by having once been hazing victims. They have been hazed; they have watched as others have been hazed; and they have waited until it's their turn to haze.

Those who claim that they enjoyed their hazing experience will tell you that they felt stronger and more powerful. They felt connected to generations of others who had experienced similar hazing and, most important, that the hazing made them feel closely bonded with a group. Whether perpetrators think that their original hazing experience was positive or negative, they know, accept, and often anticipate with glee the time that they will be able to gain control, become the leaders, and "do unto others" what was done to them.

What drives the perpetrator to be so cruel? We all have moods in which we are irritable, and sometimes we are not aware of why we are feeling that way. This happens to the perpetrators as well. Sometimes they act out things with planning and intent, and sometimes actions are driven by forces that are outside their conscious awareness. For example, traumatic experiences from the past may have involved physical or sexual abuse, humiliation, or degradation. Repressed feelings may suddenly burst forth during a hazing, and the perpetrator loses control. (Certainly, most parents have had this kind of experience while disciplining a child.) All too often, the perpetrators are intoxicated and their inhibitions are loosened, providing the perfect situation for events to become extreme and uncontrolled.

A perpetrator may be

- Identifying with authority figures or perpetrators he has known from his past, such as an authoritarian coach or father, who has treated him aggressively

- Expressing his own aggressive, sexual, or sadistic feelings, which are part of his personality, and the developmental needs of an adolescent needing to prove his masculinity

- Simply passing on a tradition that is considered sacred and special, which has been done to him and others and doesn't appear to be as dangerous as it is

- Adding something new to the hazing tradition, which adds a personal touch that may bring it into a hazardous zone

- Having a *failure of empathy*, which means that he's unable to put himself in someone else's shoes and doesn't feel or identify with what the victim is experiencing

Victims

Victims are randomly chosen participants who are recipients of hazing activities. Generally, the victims have low social status within the group, usually because they are new. At other times, the victims are the targets as defined by a particular tradition, such as the *crossing-the-line* ceremony, which has occurred in navies throughout the world since the days of the Vikings. The crossing-the-line ceremony is inflicted on a *pollywog*, a sailor that has never crossed the equator on a naval ship, by the ship's *shellbacks*, sailors who have already crossed the equator. Once the equator is crossed, a daylong strenuous and sometimes dangerous hazing ritual takes place. At the end of the hazing, the pollywog obtains the status of shellback.

Trust is a very important issue because typically individuals have chosen to be part of a group with the belief that the members are trustworthy. Athletes use the phrase "he has my back" to express their trust toward a teammate. Greeks trust their fraternity brothers as though they're part of their biological family. Though students seem to willingly participate in a variety of hazing events, they are assuming that they won't be seriously harmed by the actions of the

> ➤ **DID YOU KNOW** ≪

More than 1.5 million high school students in the United States are being subjected to some form of hazing each year. Nearly all of those hazed were humiliated. Most high school students did not perceive even the most dangerous initiation activities as hazing.[3]

group. As the hazing is occurring, the student may not identify himself as a victim.

In some cases, such as in a fraternity or sorority, students choose to join, and they accept the notion that there will be rituals attached to their pledge commitment. But they assume that these rituals will be benign. Pledges may be told that they can stop at any time, but in some cases, that isn't true. When the initiation rites are unreasonable and dangerous, the pledge may be or may perceive himself as being helpless.

A victim may be

- Identifying with the group in which he wants to gain status

- Pleasing the authority figures (for example, parents or coaches) by joining a group that they had been a member of or that will bring status to themselves or their family

- Gaining instant acceptance into the group, which also brings instant friends

- Needing a role model, which is provided by higher status members (such as a varsity player) or the group's leader (such as the coach)

- Craving structure, which provides clear rules to follow (as with a team or fraternity)

- Denying fears and insecurities, which is a method of coping with stressful situations (In denial the individual may not acknowledge his own feelings, such as fear of being alone or being different from the group. Similarly, he may deny the danger in being hazed.)

- Experiencing a moral dilemma such that the victim knows that his participation is not in sync with his own values

- Trusting the group, which is a projection of the trust that he felt in the past in other group situations, such as at home or in a class

As John Belushi said to a pledge in the film *Animal House,* "Your mistake was in trusting me."

Bystanders

Bystanders observe but usually don't actively participate in the actions taken by the perpetrators. For the most part, bystanders are those who are accepted in the group and have already been initiated. They are usually not on the same status level as the perpetrators or the victims. However, in some instances, those who are also new to the group may be bystanders, and some senior members may be bystanders. Bystanders can take many forms and consist of a wide variety of people. However, they usually are the largest portion of the group, outnumbering both the perpetrators and the victims.

In hazing, there is no such thing as an innocent bystander. Bystanders are almost always a necessary ingredient for a hazing, just as an audience is a necessary ingredient for a play. In terms of changing the nature of hazing, it is the bystanders, as a group, who have the most potential to have a substantial impact in curbing the aggression. I believe that all bystanders are affected, psychologically, by what they observe. Regardless of the type of bystander he is, or whether he willingly or accidentally participated, he is likely to have ongoing psychological effects due to his observation of the events.

There are two basic kinds of bystanders, *active* and *passive*. It's possible that the same person may experience both positions at different times, depending on his status and the internal dynamics of the group.

Active Bystanders

Active bystanders support the actions and intent of the perpetrators. They may be cheering the perpetrators by yelling "more, more" or in some way encouraging the hazing to continue. Their participation in this manner may serve to increase the perpetrators' aggression or lengthen the hazing process. Active bystanders may add to the atmosphere, heightening the emotional state. Think about a crowd at a sporting event. The athletes are spurred on by the tone and enthusiasm of the fans. This is also true during hazing incidences. We've all been active bystanders at some time in our life. We support something, such as rooting for our team or protesting some political event.

Active bystanders may or may not be totally aware of their own motivations and actions. Usually, they're not aware of the power of their presence.

An active bystander may be

- Identifying with the perpetrator, by feeling powerful and superior

- Pleasing the authority figures, by following the rules and not challenging them

- Feeling numb or disconnected emotionally and lacking empathy for the victims

- Expressing his own aggressive feelings, which have been pent up or repressed and are now given a place to be discharged

Passive Bystanders

Passive bystanders would like to blend into the wall and disappear. Usually, they identify with the victim and fear the perpetrators. They may be thinking something like, "There but for the grace of God go I." Their instinct is to run, hide, or avoid the situation, but they usually read the cues of the situation and believe that they're powerless. As one young boy in the Mepham hazing later recalled, "I was in the bunk and I laid so flat, hoping they wouldn't see me— flat and straight, hoping they wouldn't see me."[4]

Those who are passive bystanders often suffer great remorse for not intervening (also called *survivor's guilt*) and are more vulnerable to psychological problems in the future. Passive bystanders may feel uneasy because they are closer in age, size, or status to the victim and fear that they "are next." Passive bystanders may have a more highly developed sense of morality and conscience, which increases their internal conflict. They're often paralyzed by the contrast between their inner voice and the outer reality.

The passive bystander feels completely different from the active bystander. Often the passive bystander can't tolerate his position and is very sensitive to his own precarious situation, as well as the victim's dilemma. For example, during the Mepham hazing, as the victims were being brutally hazed, one of the bystanders actually started vomiting because it was so upsetting to him.

A passive bystander may be

- Identifying with the victim, feeling vulnerable and stressed

- Afraid of being victimized, because he is very aware of the power of the leaders and is afraid that the direction of the aggression can change momentarily

- Pleasing the authority figures, by accepting the activities

- Caught in a moral dilemma because he knows that the actions of the perpetrators are wrong, yet he's stuck and feels powerless to stop the activity

Supervisors

Supervisors plan, coordinate, organize, evaluate, and run the daily operations of a group activity. These people have been given the responsibility to be in charge by a higher authority, based on their knowledge, aptitude, and experience. The general expectation is that the supervisor is capable of running a program or activity for students that won't endanger their physical or psychological health. Supervisors include coaches, troop leaders, sorority sisters, and youth group coordinators.

It's important to note that most people who are either paid or volunteer to lead a group of students do so from a positive perspective. Whether they have been formally trained or not, supervisors are, in most cases, well-intentioned, good people, who care about a child's well-being.

Often supervisors see themselves as being the good guy, by working long hours and giving a tremendous amount of time and energy to the group. Some supervisors have themselves been hazed or treated disrespectfully, or they have an impulsive, aggressive temperament, all of which may come to bear on the way they supervise.

Problems, such as hazing, often arise because the supervisors aren't adequately trained or the programs are not adequately staffed to provide optimum security and safety. Supervisors may not have been aware of the hazing, or they may have been aware and had no idea of how to control it. Sometimes they send a mixed message, saying that hazing is not allowed but doing nothing to control or stop the group when it gets rowdy. This is probably the most dangerous time, because the kids read the subtext as "It's OK to haze."

Many parents have reported that their adolescents are compliant and willingly conform to strict rules imposed by their supervisor, whereas they are resistant to the limits and advice given by their own families. For example, in the mind of a developing athlete, the coach is a very important and influential person. The athlete wants to impress the coach, because the coach holds the power to the athlete's future success. It is this position of power that makes the coach or any other supervisor so significant and respected. When I first began my research about the Mepham hazing, I was struck by the way people spoke about the coach. He was a famous personality in the area. He had helped hundreds of kids become football players, including Amos Zeroue, who eventually became an NFL player. (He still is.) The coach seemed to be the most respected figure in the community. No one questioned his authority or his methods.

A supervisor may be

- A role model for the group he is supervising

- The most respected figure in the community, someone who has ultimate power and authority, which is unchecked by administrators or the community

- Pleasing higher authority figures by perpetuating the status quo; for example, allowing a tradition to continue, even though it may be hazing

- Identifying with an authority figure, like his own father, his own coach, or another significant person

- Gaining ego gratification, which means his self-esteem is being strengthened by his role as a supervisor

Perhaps one of the driving forces in being a coach is the satisfaction derived from creating winners, whether it be an athletic team, cheerleaders, or a band.

Administrators

Administrators are the highest authority. They establish the group or program, choose the supervisors, and create policy, guidelines, and training mandates. Administrators are responsible for running the show, for seeing the big picture, for making sure that all the parts of the organization are working in harmony and that those beneath them, such as supervisors, are capable and will carry out their duties as expected. Administrators include high school superintendents, presidents of national Greek organizations, supervisors of church groups, and leaders of club athletics.

There are over one million people caring for our high school children in terms of athletic, art, drama, and musical activities. This number does not include other kinds of religious groups or supervisors in colleges, such as fraternity or sorority presidents. It is therefore impossible to discuss the various circumstances of supervision and administration that may occur. However, based on the amount of hazardous hazing over the last several years, it seems likely that there is insufficient training and control by authorities over the supervisors and students.

Administrators are often friendly with those who've been in the organization and may not be able to view internal problems without prejudice. For example, if the town loves a winning coach, but the coach has a bad temper, he may be tolerated by the administration, even if that is not in the best interests of the athletes.

An administrator may be

- Protecting his reputation and the reputation of the organization

- Maintaining the status quo, by choosing not to institute changes

- Lacking awareness or ability to change the system

Community

The community is the much larger group, such as a village, parish, town, or city, where the hazing has occurred. The community has a responsibility to demand appropriate controls from the administration. But it also has the responsibility to be part of the system of checks and balances. If the community blindly supports a leader, coach, or supervisor, it may be helping to set the stage for a hazardous hazing. It is possible that the community as a whole does not understand its power.

A community may be

- Identifying with a winning team, which brings status to the community

- Providing special privileges to parents, teachers, leaders, and coaches of key players, which helps maintain the status quo

- Expecting awards that reflect positively on the town, which may increase property values and town prestige

WHY DOES HAZING OCCUR AND HOW DOES IT BECOME HAZARDOUS?

I initially started my research into hazing with two questions: Why and how?

Why would high school kids hurt one another in the way they did in the Mepham, New York, case, and how does hazing move from teasing and horseplay to acts of extreme violence and sexual abuse?

There are no easy answers to these questions. Kids can and do haze, even if it is against the law or the school policy, even if they know better, even if they didn't like it when it happened to them, and even if they know that it may severely hurt another person. However, there *are* answers. While interviewing parents and students involved in hazing, I began to see patterns emerge that helped explain why and how hazing occurs. We'll first start with the why and then tackle the how.

Why Does Hazing Occur?

Simply put, as human beings, we have an innate need to belong to groups. Groups provide us with a sense of safety, a feeling of belonging to something bigger and stronger than ourselves, or they may connect us with others of similar interests and tastes. Groups can also bolster our social status and credibility with family, friends, and peers.

Every group has a process in which it accepts or rejects its members. In some groups, the process is a tradition that has been passed down for many years. When this tradition or initiation rite becomes solidified, it may include hazing, proving that the new member is able to withstand physical and emotional stress and proving that the new member is worthy of inclusion in the group. For some groups, this proof of worthiness is the key to being accepted and the only way to become a member.

One of the interesting aspects of hazing is that the senior group members feel that it is their right and duty to pass on the tradition, even if it involves painful and illegal hazing traditions. In fact, many kids actually expect some sort of hazing to happen, although they rarely expect it to be so severe and dangerous as many of the examples used in this chapter. They definitely don't picture themselves as being severely hurt. When the hazing occurs, it feels like it is a case of bait and switch—that they expected one thing and got another. In many cases, what they get is a hazardous hazing.

How Does Hazing Skid into the Hazardous Zone?

To understand how a hazing can turn hazardous, it's helpful to think about the severity of the weather and other natural events. Meteorologists coined the term the *perfect storm* to explain a particularly deadly storm that occurred on the New England coast in 1991. Very specific elements merged in order to create the extreme chaos of the perfect storm. Perhaps the most powerful element was the energy that drove the storm, an energy that we sometimes witness when there is a powerful nor'easter, a hurricane, or a tsunami. It is as though the energy is being stored somewhere in the earth's core and it needs to be released.

Meteorologists try to determine if certain conditions are occurring that are more likely to create significantly threatening weather conditions and other possible perfect storms. They study the wind currents, the temperature, and the degree of humidity. They study current conditions throughout the country as well as irregular weather patterns or geological events. When two wind currents, one hot and the other cold, are likely to collide, the conditions for a storm become evident. As the specifics are determined, the perfect storm may be created, a storm that often packs the force of a lethal blow.

The same thing can happen with hazing. If the right elements all come together at the same time, a tradition can become hazardous, causing significant physical and psychological damage. I call this theory the *perfect storm of hazardous hazing*.

The elements that make up this perfect storm include the following:

1. Dynamics of the group, where there is a defined and strict hierarchy.

2. An emotional state of the group that is aroused, aggressive, or rowdy.

3. An available time and space. An unsupervised or under-supervised location coupled with enough time to complete the acts.

4. An attitude toward authority. Students are conditioned not to question the authority figure. They are taught to do as they are told and just take it.

5. Individual personalities of victims, bystanders, and perpetrators. The specific mix of personalities may encourage aggressive behaviors.

6. Traditions or initiation rites that have become dangerous through time but may not be distinguished as more dangerous than usual.

7. The natural desire for students to want to prove their worthiness to the group, by participating in questionable activities

in order to prove themselves, please leaders and peers, and be accepted.

8. The natural developmental needs of adolescents that urge them to explore their new physical selves, including aggressive emotions and sexual feelings.

9. A no pain–no gain attitude, usually found in team sports and Greek organizations. Students are taught to endure pain and punishment (a take-one-for-the-team mentality) while simultaneously encouraged to unleash aggression on opponents and foes.

10. Unconscious mechanisms that allow adolescents to identify with their leaders. Students may be unconsciously compelled to repeat their traumatic experience (such as a hazing) in order to feel in control. They undo the humiliation that they originally experienced by humiliating others. This psychological process seems to help them feel whole again.

It is possible that a mix of any of these elements can cause hazings to skid out of control. The more we're aware of what causes a hazing to become hazardous, the better we will be able to prevent a future dangerous situation from occurring. For a more detailed and in-depth discussion of the theory *perfect storm of hazardous hazing*, please visit my Web site at www.insidehazing.com.

Just like the perfect storm in nature, where disparate elements came together to form a powerful and devastating storm, a hazardous hazing requires conditions of the physical and social environment, characteristics of the individual and group, and internal processes of the individual to come together in a similarly sinister way. When these elements are set and the emotional energy is available, the likelihood of a hazardous hazing is increased. However, there are ways to prevent these events from happening. We will look at those in the next chapter.

2

Preventing Hazing

In October 2002, Jake Savoy was a sophomore on the Gators, the football team of St. Amant High School. St. Amant, a tiny town situated halfway between New Orleans and Baton Rouge, Louisiana, is a place where high school football is embedded in the fabric of the community.

It was Jake's birthday, and it was celebrated the way it always had been done, with a birthday "whooping," as they call it. Certainly, a smack on the tush is not unusual, but on this day, the football team's tradition took a new spin. As Jake entered the locker room after a long workout, he was stripped naked, taped to a bench, and then the beating began. The hazing was orchestrated by a teammate who sat by Jake's head and told the players how many hits they could have. One by one, his teammates hit him with open hands and a sandal. One boy shoved his buttocks in Jake's face and shoulder. Another took the now-empty roll of athletic tape and stuck it in his buttocks, like a birthday candle. Jake's rear was covered in blood blisters. The bruising would show up later.

Unfortunately, stories like Jake's are becoming more common in the world of teenagers. Traditions and initiation rites in groups such as fraternities and sororities, athletic and cheerleading teams, and even church groups, are more degrading and dangerous than they were just ten years ago. Many teens involved in a hazing believe that what was done to them was normal or just part of growing up. Others feel powerless to stop the hazing tradition or are afraid to confront the hazers. Most hazing goes unreported for these very reasons.

However, a really remarkable thing happened in Jake's case. After his hazing, Jake, on his own, marched into the coach's office and quit the team, saying, "I had enough of this birthday thing." Jake knew that what happened was not right and unlike most other kids, he wasn't going to take any more, and he wasn't going to let it go unaddressed.

How can we teach our children and students to behave and act as Jake did? How do we help them stand up for themselves and prevent future hazing? Jake, a thin, wiry underclassman had no power next to a team full of older, bigger, and stronger boys. He did, however, recognize that no one had the right to treat him that way. He learned this from his mother, who early on, instilled in him the knowledge that no one, not even a family member, had the right to violate his body.

Karen, his mom, had taught him that it was *his* body, and he had a right and duty to protect it. Later, as a preteen, Jake remembered that his mom gave him an article to read about hazing. They discussed it, and although it did not save him from being hazed, it did have an impact. These early childhood lessons, updated with relevant information, served Jake well. It gave him the understanding and the courage to stand up and report the hazing.

All of us must teach our children about whom to trust and what is acceptable behavior. Karen Savoy taught Jake to respect and protect his body, a lesson that was deeply embedded in his unconscious. If we teach our children what "feels right and wrong," they carry that feeling inside for the rest of their lives. In addition, Karen kept open lines of communication through Jake's teen years. By being involved in all his sports and academic activities, showing up at his games, having his uniform ready, and being there for the trips to the orthopedist, Karen demonstrated her commitment to her son. Jake unconsciously integrated his mother's messages and maintained open communication, even when it was embarrassing or difficult.

We can all have this impact on our children and students, if we make the commitment. To help, here are four ways to prevent hazing in our homes, schools, and communities:

1. Create a trusting relationship.
2. Educate yourself.
3. Educate your kids.
4. Question authority figures.

CREATE A TRUSTING RELATIONSHIP

Although the Beatles song says "All You Need Is Love," the truth is that love is often not enough. You need a way to communicate with your child, and building a system of communication is not an easy thing to do. Adolescents need to test their limits by seeing how far they can go before getting in trouble. So it may be hard to show them love and understanding when you believe they also need discipline.

In a way, adolescents are like caterpillars in the process of becoming butterflies. Teens are half in and half out of their cocoon, struggling to develop and learn how to fly. Simultaneously, parents often fear the adolescent's drive for freedom and independence. Parents may respond by increasing controls and setting limits on what their children can and cannot do. Sometimes parents invade the adolescent's physical and personal space. These conflicting needs and power struggles may hamper your ability to talk and feel close to your child, especially when they need you most, when they are in the turbulent waters of pre-adolescence and adolescence (middle and high school).

Coaches and teachers are often the adults that kids turn to when they are in conflict with their own parents. They have tremendous power to influence those teens with whom they have a relationship. When they use their power positively, they can change a kid's life. In order to help teens deal with stressful situations, such as hazing, I've developed a few techniques, which are discussed in the following sections.

Communicating with Your Kids

Building and maintaining a trusting relationship is the most important aspect of parenting. It begins the moment the baby is born. As parents, you protect and nurture him, holding him in a way that he can feel secure, answering his cries so that he knows you're available to him. We try to create a foundation to build and maintain an open and trusting relationship with our children. This is done by spending time talking to our children about things other than picking up their toys or doing their homework. Today's parents have fewer opportunities to build these kinds of teaching moments, because both the parents and the kids are overscheduled. Two techniques that might help are

- Special Time
- Special Signals

Special Time

From early childhood through adolescence, parents need to carve out *special time* for each child. This special time, given by each parent, may be only ten to fifteen minutes, three times a week, but it is designated "special time." This regularly scheduled time promises the child that you won't do anything else during that time. You will not answer the phone, or read the mail, or deal with the other kids. Instead you will be completely focused on that particular child.

During special time, the child chooses an activity to do with the parent and the parent creates an invisible shield, to protect the intimacy of the special time. As you play, whether it is catching a ball, playing cards, or drawing, you should be completely attentive to the child's communications. It is during these special times that the bond, the trust, the sense that you are there for him, no matter what, will be communicated and reinforced.

These special times should be punctuated by *special days*, when each child is given a longer period of time to do something special with each parent. Later in life, children may not remember the specifics, but they will remember the special feeling of having a full day to spend with their parent, not competing for the parent's attention, simply being indulged by spending that time together. Special time affords the parent the opportunity to teach important lessons about mind and body, about what is acceptable and what is not. It also teaches the child that he has someone to turn to when he's feeling uncomfortable, stressed, or scared.

In adolescence, it becomes more difficult to relate to your child. This is a normal event and marks the child's entrance into the real world, a world that they must learn to negotiate without you. But the parent can still request (and sometimes get) those special times and special days, even from an adolescent. For example, a girl might want to shop somewhere special or far away from her peers. A boy might want to go to a ball game or a car show. These one-on-one activities give the parent the time and space to maintain the open communication that's necessary for a trusting and secure relationship.

Special Signals

Arming our children with many ways to communicate is always helpful. *Special signals* are used to alert a parent that the child is feeling uncomfortable, even if the child can't say it directly. Kids should pick a word or phrase that sounds usual but has a special meaning to only the parent and child. The phrase is a substitute for "Help, get me out of here!" The code is necessary, especially in pre-adolescence and adolescence, when kids need to "save face" with their friends but also need parental intervention.

For example, your high school freshman daughter has been invited to a party where there will be juniors and seniors. She feels honored to be invited to such a party but also fears it, expecting alcohol and older boys to be present. Of course, she does not tell you her fears prior to the party, so you might even encourage her to go. After an hour or two at the party, she feels intimidated by the older boys, who are drunk and begin hitting on her. She calls and gives you the special word or phrase that the two of you had already established, such as "This party is excellent." The word *excellent* is the special word that means "Help! I'm feeling pressured or uncomfortable and I need your support; help me get out of this situation." You then respond with a "cover story," in which you state that there is a family emergency and you must pick her up immediately.

The moment you pick her up is a very special time. She is most probably a little freaked out and wants to tell you what was happening. By being positive and supportive, you reinforce the fact that you are proud that she called and that you will always be there. Don't give her a lecture about parties and use scare tactics. You want to show her that she can confide in you and be supported.

Each time a child uses this signal, she is relying on you, trusting you to help her maneuver through difficult times. Surprisingly, adolescents rely on this signal more frequently than you might imagine. They still need their parents as guides and for emotional support. However, as in the example here, kids want to initiate the help rather than having the parent intervene.

Signals can be difficult to read. As parents, we may need to push and prod our children to do things they aren't comfortable with. We can't tell when a child is afraid to move ahead, to try new things, and to face uncomfortable situations. We can't tell when he's being confronted with an overwhelmingly difficult situation. However, the special signal can help the parent know when things are truly an emergency.

As parents, we tend to focus on what *we think* is important, what *we want* our children to learn. However, we must be vigilant to hear *what they need.* We must read between the lines and hear what they are *not* saying, their nonverbal messages. To do this, we must be open and accepting, listening and responding to their agenda, not only ours. If you establish that the signal is to be used in times of real danger, such as when one uses 9-1-1, it will help both child and parent.

Teachers and coaches can use this same kind of system. At the beginning of the school year or coaching season, the teacher or coach can create a special word or visual signal to be used by any student when something serious is happening. This gives the student the message that teachers and coaches are open and interested in their thoughts and feelings, especially the significantly distressing ones.

In the Mepham hazing, discussed in Chapter One, the coach wondered why none of the athletes had whispered to him, "Hey coach, check out bunk thirteen." The answer is that they were probably intimidated and thought that such type of communication was neither possible nor encouraged. In order for athletes to feel comfortable informing an adult of questionable behavior, the adult must set the stage for that type of communication. Adults need to signal, in verbal and nonverbal ways, that they would rather hear the communication, even if it is uncomfortable, than have it buried. Kids tend to stop talking in order to avoid making an adult uncomfortable, unless they have been repeatedly told, by parents, teachers, and coaches, "Telling is better than not telling."

Communicating with Your Students

As teachers and coaches, you begin building and maintaining a trusting relationship the moment you meet your students. Kids hear what you say as well as how you say it, and they can instantly determine what kind of teacher or coach you are. If you want your students to trust and respect you, you must demonstrate trust and respect for each of them.

Creating a relationship with each child is necessary. They must feel that your job is to nurture their growth and development and that your main focus is to help them. You need to establish a safe environment, in which communication is encouraged. Remember, you are tremendously important in the eyes of your students. They listen attentively to you and seek your approval. You have the power to influence them.

➤ DID YOU KNOW ◄

In a study I conducted in 2005 with high school and college students and their parents, 83 percent thought that coaches of athletic teams have tremendous power over their students, and 70 percent of the students viewed their coach as a father figure. These statistics show that coaches can have a tremendous influence on their students and teams when it comes to hazing prevention.

As a teacher or coach, you can communicate with your students in two significant ways: directly, through meetings and private conversations, and indirectly, through nonverbal signals. When used thoughtfully and intelligently, both can dramatically affect your relationship with the student and your ability to help prevent hazing.

Team Meetings and Private Conversations

Communicating with your students through team or class meetings and private mini-meetings can be very powerful. Both can go a long way toward creating a trusting relationship and laying the groundwork for getting the kind of undivided attention that you may need to talk about rules and expectations related to hazing.

1. *Team or class meeting.* This is the most common form of communication, in which a coach or teacher directly states procedures and expectations. It is a good idea to distribute a written statement that includes the following:

- Explain regulations, requirements, and expectations for the team or class. This should include specific rules and expectations on hazing.

- Outline how they can contact you. Include phone numbers for your office, home, and cell phone. If you have e-mail, include that as well.

- Outline when they can contact you. This should be as welcoming and specific as possible. Remember, you want your student to feel comfortable contacting you with problems or emergencies. Give examples of potential emergencies (including hazing) that students should contact you about.

2. *Private conversations or mini-meetings.* These are individual, private meetings between coach or teacher and student. Many times, these conversations will be informal and spontaneous. The purpose of a mini-meeting is to

- Strengthen the bond between the coach or teacher and student. A quick talk after a game or in between classes can go a long way in establishing a positive relationship and teaching about sportsmanship and leadership.

- Provide support and positive reinforcement when possible. Praise is never remembered as well as criticism, so finding positive attributes and telling students about their contribution to the group is highly recommended.

- Encourage communication, especially if something is wrong. Most students feel more comfortable talking in these informal, private meetings. Encourage them to approach you whenever they need to.

- Reiterate your expectations of the student. If you think a student is having trouble with the rules or expectations of the group, let him know.

- Initiate planned and spontaneous mini-meetings with each student. This is especially important with those who have leadership skills and are able to influence the group.

Nonverbal Signals

Nonverbal signals are another significant method of communication, and we're often unaware of their power. People use nonverbal signals to express a wide range of emotions and to express hidden meanings. Political advisers and advertisers often use nonverbal messages to their advantage. The color of the tie of the President of the United States is used to communicate strength. Advertisers use youthful imagery and edgy music to promote products to teenagers. In the same way, a coach's stance, arms crossed, legs planted firmly, may communicate "I'm in charge."

The power of nonverbal communication in hazing is significant. Hazing has occurred for generations, and it's a kind of behavior that's been tolerated or encouraged, directly and indirectly. When teachers and coaches give off signals that indicate hazing traditions are not a big deal, they are sending a direct message to all of their students.

I often hear adults reminisce about hazing with a smile on their face, nodding their head and laughing, as they think about "the best times of their lives." Here is where nonverbal communication can become dangerous. On one level, adults may not want to stop their students from having similar experiences, thinking it's all part of growing up. But they may also know that hazing can have devastating consequences and can leave a student scarred for life. These mixed messages can leave a student confused. Here is where parents, teachers, and coaches are most vulnerable, because they say no verbally, but their nonverbal cues are really saying, "It's not so bad to haze." It's so important that we become more attentive, alert, and aware of the nonverbal signals we're giving.

It's important to notice your own nonverbal signals, but sometimes kids give nonverbal signals as well. Be aware of what a student is not saying as much as what he is saying. Note the nonverbal cues that he is sending. Once you have picked up on such communication, try to create a bridge so that you can discover what is going on and then intervene accordingly.

Many people wondered how the victims in the Mepham, New York, hazing incident were playing football each day, as they were being beaten and sodomized day and night. One would imagine that the way the victims would run, move, or perhaps avoid eye contact would have been evident to the coaches. These are nonverbal cues that teachers and coaches are expected to notice.

In fact, the head coach of the Mepham football team referred to one of the victims as "Gatorade" because he was frequently asking for the drink. As the coach told this story, it seemed that he was aware that the boy was trying to make contact. He wondered why the freshman had been coming around so often. Unfortunately, the coach hadn't connected the dots, hadn't realized that something was wrong with the student. Perhaps, had he been more attentive to his own feelings and signals as well as to this child's (who was a victim), he would have increased the contact with that boy and learned about the hazing events.

As a parent, teacher, or coach, you have significant influence on students and simultaneously tremendous responsibility. You must be aware of your own verbal and nonverbal communication, as well as being alert to those kinds of communications from kids. I know this isn't easy. However, it is vital that your message about hazing is loud and clear. In many cases, it is your tone and your rules that can stamp out hazing. Mastering the way you communicate with your children and students is essential in preventing hazing.

EDUCATE YOURSELF

Congratulations! You've already taken a giant step by being interested enough to read this book. But that's just the first step. The more involved you get in learning, the more likely you are to prevent hazing. See the Resource Guide at the back of the book for other books, Web sites, and movies that will help you learn more about what you can do to prevent hazing.

Educating yourself also means that you need to understand and identify the behaviors that encourage hazing. Take a long look in the mirror—the one that reflects your actions and values—and check to see what messages you're sending. Are they aggressive or abusive? For example, in St. Amant, Louisiana, a football coach reprimanded an athlete who had missed a play. In front of a stadium full of fans, the coach screamed at him, yelled obscenities, and violently yanked his head by grabbing the mouth guard on his helmet. The player's mom could be heard yelling above the din, "Give it to him coach, you're right!" Many of the other parents were shocked by both the coach and the mother. The lesson being sent to that player and to the team was this: it's OK to be abusive.

It's important for you to consider your own attitude toward hazing. It's likely that hazing is occurring and has been occurring in your community, though it's not recognized as such. Often parents will actually say, "Oh, I did that, no big deal." Men, in particular, often diminish the harm in the "pranks" and initiation rites that they either endured or perpetuated. They believe that being able to tolerate the hazing traditions proves that they're strong and masculine.

Even in Jake Savoy's family, after Jake had been hazed, his father naively denied his own experience of being hazed. He then told this story: "When I was on the football team, they put Icy Hot in my jockstrap. But that was no big deal, 'cause all I did was run into the showers and wash it off." Jake's dad didn't recognize that he had been hazed, that his private parts had been harmed. He felt that because it wasn't permanent, it wasn't hazardous hazing. But that is not the truth. Though Jerry's experience was less aggressive than Jake's experience, Jerry was humiliated and his body was harmed.

If you are a teacher or coach, you must evaluate your own stance on hazing, which means recognizing your teaching and coaching styles. Are you authoritarian, making rigid rules and harshly punishing students? Are you completely laid back, giving little direction and not much control to the team or class? Did you realize that both the authoritarian and laid-back styles often encourage or allow hazing rituals to continue?

Your goal should be to become more compromising. A compromising teacher or coach sets rules yet creates a dialogue with the students and compromises when necessary. Use some of the communication techniques discussed earlier in this chapter. Knowing who you are, and how that might allow hazing to occur is vital to you and to your students.

Educating yourself about hazing also means acknowledging the cues that you send to students. Take a long hard look at the ways you communicate, both verbally and nonverbally. For example, coaches who seem authoritarian and distant are sending a message to their athletes that communication is not encouraged. In some sports, such as football, films are taken on a daily basis and are used as a teaching tool for the athletes. The coaches should also be filmed so that they can evaluate their own behaviors during practices and games. Seeing yourself "in action" can be very beneficial. As they say, a picture is worth a thousand words.

EDUCATE YOUR KIDS

Hazing doesn't usually occur before age twelve. I don't think kids are ready to understand hazing until they are at the end of middle school or about twelve or thirteen. So definitions and examples of hazing shouldn't be emphasized before that age. Giving kids this kind of information before they are ready to understand and integrate it is fruitless and potentially harmful. However, by eighth grade, all students should be learning about hazing, learning how to recognize it, and learning how to respond to it.

Parents, teachers, and coaches need to discuss hazing. They need to underline the personal responsibility to protect oneself, the team, or group and to report events that have been witnessed. When articles on hazing appear in magazines, in the newspaper, or on the Internet, it is important to have your child read them. If a hazing occurs in or near your community, take that as a good opportunity for you to discuss it. Your openness about the events will signal that your children can feel free to question and understand.

Most kids, especially boys, won't take hazing seriously. In the Mepham, New York, hazing (described in Chapter One), even after the brutality of the hazing was evident, many of the students thought it "was funny." They really meant, "This is very uncomfortable for me to discuss, and I need to deny the implications of these acts." They feel uneasy because they can't tolerate the thought that this might have happened to them. It's difficult to penetrate an adolescent's mind, but it's not impossible.

Teachers and coaches may not feel as compassionately as I do about the importance of preventing hazing. You may have experienced hazing on many levels, having been hazed or hazing others. You may feel that it is an integrated part of the culture of your town or sport. Nonetheless, as a significant role model, you are given responsibility to take care of the minds and bodies of all your students and will be held responsible for the consequences of a hazing, even if you had no knowledge of it. It is imperative that the tone you set when teaching about hazing is serious.

Many students report that anti-hazing lectures have been given with a "wink, wink" added—meaning, "Even though I say 'don't,' I mean 'do.'" This mixed message is a real dilemma for all adults. We have been adolescents and have done many of the things that we tell our children to avoid. If we forbid them to engage in activities that we did, we feel like hypocrites. Instead, many times we ignore or deny their behaviors and undermine our own efforts to prevent hazardous hazing.

It is important to be clear and firm, yet understanding, when talking about hazing. The following lessons should be taught to all children and students:

1. *No one has the right to touch, degrade, humiliate, or cause any kind of pain or suffering to your body, no matter who they are, or what they promise, or what they threaten.* This is a basic principle that should be instilled in each child, using age-appropriate language. Though adolescents will not want to hear adults discuss this, because it comes too close to their budding sexuality, they *will* listen (even if they make every attempt not to). I advise parents, teachers, and coaches to use a technique that I use with resistant adolescents. Throw enough mud on the wall and some of it is bound to stick. Loosely translated, that means, keep trying to send the message, and have faith that something will be remembered.

2. *Everyone involved in a hazing may be held responsible for the consequences.* Perpetrators will be held responsible, and the consequences may range from detention or suspension to harsh punishments like probation or even prison. Bystanders can also be held responsible and suffer the consequences for not reporting the hazing. Even teachers, coaches, and other kinds of administrators may be held responsible for hazing. Victims, of course, are not responsible for the consequences of a hazing.

3. *If you report a hazing, you are a hero.* Reporting, even anonymously, is better than not reporting. The life you save may one day be your own.

4. *Everyone and anyone is a potential victim.* Don't believe that because you have a special relationship with the perpetrators or other members of the group, you will not be victimized. *Nothing protects you.*

5. *If you are a victim, you did not cause your victimization.* Most victims in a hazing are chosen randomly. You didn't do anything to mark yourself as someone to be victimized. Remember, *it is not your fault.*

6. *If you are a bystander, you may not have participated, but you have been affected.* You need to understand how the hazing may have changed you. It is likely that professional psychological help would be good for you.

7. *If you are a perpetrator, whether or not you have been reported, you are affected by your actions.* Psychological intervention is recommended. Continuing to intimidate bystanders and victims may increase your legal consequences should the hazing be discovered. The fact that you may have been a victim in a previous hazing and merely continued the tradition is not a viable legal defense; although, it is relevant psychologically.

8. *Regardless of promises to the contrary, specific hazing techniques may be used.* If an athletic team, fraternity, or youth group has used hazing techniques in the past, there is a very good chance they will use those same techniques (or worse) with you.

9. *You are not a stronger, better, tougher person by participating in a hazing.* Athletic teams and fraternities and sororities often state that the hazing process proves your abilities and how tough you are. Though the initiation process may be grueling, you are not a better or stronger person for having suffered through it.

10. *No matter what you think, hazing has a deep psychological effect on you.* Even if the hazing is never discovered, you will carry around the events in your memory for the rest of your life. There is something deeply emotional about hazing, and it sticks to your insides.

QUESTION AUTHORITY FIGURES

Question authority figures? This may sound strange coming from a psychologist and devoted mother. However, questioning authority is an important lesson our kids need to learn to grow into successful, mature adults. It's equally important in preventing hazing. The

---

An Insider's View of Hazing

We teach our children to be wary about strangers, drugs, and alcohol. We teach them about sex and not to drive drunk, but we never think to teach them about hazing. We encourage our children to join sports teams as a safe way to occupy their time; never do we consider what really goes on in the locker room. We encourage them to join the same fraternity or sorority that we did or that we wished we could have. We believe that it is a safe place, a band of brothers, a positive experience. Never do we realize that the act of joining can end in death. We spend an enormous amount of time and money finding the right college, never realizing that the schools don't really provide a safe and secure environment for our children. Never do we consider that as we send them off to college to begin to prepare to be adults, that drinking, partying, and hazing can be a huge part of this experience and that it can be deadly.

—MICHAEL AND LESLIE, parents of freshman pledge who died due to a hazing

---

trick is teaching our kids when such behavior is appropriate and how it can be used to protect them from harm.

In this day and age, each and every person is liable for his or her own actions. We're held accountable for what we do and even what we don't do. (For example, as a psychologist, I can be held responsible for not reporting child abuse.) It's important for everyone to take responsibility and know when and how to question authority figures.

Simply put, we need to teach our kids to question authority figures because authority figures are not always right. After all, I bet there are times when you question an authority in your own work and personal life. It could be a boss or colleague at work, a physician whose diagnosis you question by seeking a second opinion, or a mechanic working on your car. All of us have had the experience, sometimes uncomfortable, of questioning an authority that has more power, seniority, or knowledge than we do.

The news is constantly filled with stories of authorities behaving badly. From large corporations, such as Enron and WorldCom, to individuals, such as Bobby Knight, Martha Stewart, and Rafael Palmeiro, many prominent authority figures have admitted to or have been found guilty of wrongdoing. How do we teach students not to imitate these behaviors?

First, our job is to be good role models, by doing what is right and honest. As parents, teachers, and coaches, we are the people who show kids how to behave. If we want them to uphold specific behaviors and values, we must teach it to them by modeling the behaviors. The most significant learning occurs via imitation and assimilation.

We need to teach kids, when appropriate, to question sources of information, to question individuals in power, and to think for themselves. Children, students, and athletes must learn *when* to question authority figures and *how* to question them. The entire issue needs to be thoroughly and repeatedly discussed and taught.

When kids learn to haze, they are doing so with the overt or covert permission of authority figures—whether it's coaches, team captains, or fraternity brothers. They're allowing themselves to break from their own individual value system and follow authorities, who may be physically or psychologically intimidating. We must arm them, teach them in advance, not at the time of crisis, what to do in such circumstances. After all, we don't wait till there's a fire to teach kids what to do in a fire!

When to Question Authority Figures

Let's consider some ways to teach your child or student when to question authority figures. From your own personal experiences or those from the news, there are always situations in which one feels that an authority figure is wrong. Rather than simply grumbling about it, present the situation to the family, class, or team and encourage a healthy discussion, highlighting any points that you think are important.

In a family, parents might discuss a situation where they experienced some prejudice due to race, religion, or socioeconomic class. A teacher might bring up a dilemma that is relevant to current events or have the class do a project that challenges the status quo. The coach might refer to professional athletes or coaches who acted inappropriately and ask the team what they think they'd have done if they'd witnessed the situation. The adult needs to emphasize the importance of the individual making a personal judgment and then, if necessary, finding a way to stop the abuse and communicate the problem effectively.

One of the most important aspects of parenting, teaching, and coaching is being a role model. Children do as we do, not as we say. So if you are smoker but you say, "don't smoke," your kids are still likely to smoke. In the same way, if we model behaviors that demonstrate positive group dynamics, we are modeling the kind of behavior we want our children to do. A good example of this can be seen in the following story.

A baseball coach in New York carried a lot of weight in his community, not because he was well-trained or fair but because he intimidated everyone. He yelled at the kids and humiliated those that did not perform. He had his older son act as umpire and somehow his team always won, regardless of their true performance and skills. He was also in charge of picking the elite team that would engage in serious competition.

On one occasion, he kept his team on an open field during a thunderstorm, as all the parents watched in fear, imagining a bolt of lightning hitting a player. Finally, one parent said, "If we teach our kids never to be in an open field during a thunderstorm, why are we letting them do it now? We are teaching them to stay in a dangerous situation." That mother got the other parents to march out to the field, in the pouring rain, and take their kids home. The coach protested, but the parents overruled. Subsequently, the parents banded together and spoke with the baseball commissioner about this coach's behaviors. The coach was alerted, an assistant coach was added, and the situation improved.

The most important lesson in this example is that the parents banded together to question the coach during a potentially dangerous situation. This was an important demonstration for their children. The parents modeled when to question authority. By explaining why and how the parents banded together, they're teaching their children when and how to respond whenever they're in a similar situation.

How to Question Authority Figures

It is not good enough to tell kids to follow their gut and not obey instructions. If there's a reason to question an authority, we must also teach our children appropriate methods to do so. In hazing-related events, the choices range from group encounters with the authority figure to a private face-to-face meeting between the student and the authority to anonymous or public methods of questioning authorities.

Authority figures may include the captain of the team, the president of the fraternity, the coach, or the bandleader. Most students have been trained to be respectful, follow orders, and do as they're told. It is this kind of compliance and blind obedience that creates a perfect scenario for hazing to occur. We need to teach our children and students when to comply and when to question, because ultimately, they can't simply claim that the leader said so. They will be held personally responsible for their actions, and they need to think before they act.

Forming a group is usually the safest, most effective way to question an authority figure, especially during a hazing. Students should be encouraged to seek others when appropriate. As in the previous example, about the parents questioning the baseball coach, there is usually safety and power in numbers. Here are some suggestions:

- Everyone within your group should agree to the action that is about to happen. You have power as a group because you have strength in numbers.

- If you are being victimized or feel threatened, simply leave. This means, leave as a group and go somewhere you feel safe. Stay in the group to make sure that each one of you is OK and that there is no longer a threat.

- If a hazing is occurring to others, and your group wants to intervene and inhibit the perpetrators, do so in the safest way possible. If they can be reasoned with, remind them of legal consequences that they might suffer or that the entire team, group, or fraternity might be disbanded. If the group is large enough, have some members stop the perpetrators while the other members try to help the victims.

- If the group is not able to intervene, then exit, as a group, and contact authorities. You can do this anony-mously if you prefer.

If you or your child can't round up a group, the communication should still occur. However, this may be very difficult to accomplish during a hazing. In cases when your child or student is being threat-ened or victimized, the best defense is simply to leave. After a threatening incident, try to report the event to the supervisor that you and your child trust or have the closest relationship with. (More specifics about this are found in Chapter Four.)

When your child talks with a supervisor or another adult about the hazing, make sure your child knows the following:

- Approach the authority figure with respect, not hostil-ity, and without being defensive. Have your questions and issues prioritized in your mind. Decide in advance what your goal is and what information you want to provide or receive. After the meeting, write down as many details as you can. Include the date and place of the meeting. Tell someone you trust, like your parents, about the meeting, before and after.

- Depending on the subject and solutions, you can write a letter or e-mail, thanking the authority figure for his time, and reiterate the solutions that were agreed upon by the two of you.

- You can also choose to question the situation anonymously. To do this, you need to use the methods that are provided by the school or institution, such as a suggestion box or an online site. Cornell University created a hazing information site for their students at hazing.cornell.edu; other schools use mysafecampus.com or reporti-it.com. The Mothers Against School Hazing site (MASHinc.org) also contains a hazing-reporting function. (Please see the Resource Guide at the end of the book for more information on these organizations.)

- You might choose not to speak directly to the authority figure but to someone in a position above him, but still within the same group, such as the athletic director, rather than your coach. You might do this because you believe it will be the most efficient or safest method. If you choose this method, you can do so anonymously; however, the more information you provide, the more likely you will be taken seriously. This also helps those investigating to do a thorough job, which will bring the hazing to a halt.

- Last but not least, you can turn to local media—either personally or anonymously (more about media contact in Chapter Four).

As adults, we can't expect behaviors from kids that we don't expect from ourselves. Before we can expect students to prevent hazing, we must prevent it in any way possible ourselves. As with most problems in adolescence, the key to prevention and intervention begins with a good adult-child relationship, marked by open communication.

Detecting the Warning Signs

Steve, a six-foot tall, dark, and handsome eighteen-year-old, left for college in late August. He and some elementary school friends from his old neighborhood were going to the same state university, about a four-hour drive from his house. Although this was Steve's first time away from home, he was clear about his direction and his values, and he felt secure about his identity. He knew that he didn't want to join a fraternity and assured his mother that he wouldn't do so.

Steve instantly loved college. He seemed to have no period of adjustment, no homesickness, no qualms about being on his own. He made friends quickly and was going to parties "downtown." Although he gave up many childhood friends for the new people he was meeting, his mother was thrilled with his instant adjustment and immediately became less anxious about her older son going off to college. Steve called his mother almost daily and all the reports were great.

At Christmas break, Steve's mother felt that he was somehow different, but she couldn't exactly define how. They had always had a very close, deeply emotional relationship, in which she spoke honestly and encouraged him to do the same. In fact, Steve spoke openly to both his parents and his younger brother. However, things seemed to be changing.

In January, Steve decided to go back to college a bit early, and his mother found him distant. He suddenly announced that he wouldn't be calling every day, but just once a week, and she wasn't allowed to call him. Steve began to call on Sundays. He was brief and distant, sounding tired, and always hanging up quickly with a snarly "gotta go."

In March, the phone rang around 2:30 A.M., Steve was in the local hospital, but he assured his mother he was OK. He said he had slipped while fooling around with some friends and had hurt his finger. These events had taken place the previous day. Steve's mom was wondering why he was in the hospital at 2:30 A.M. if the incident had happened thirty-six hours previously. Due to some issues about insurance, a nurse called Steve's mom the next day and mentioned that Steve wasn't alone, that there were at least six boys, and that there were varying degrees of injury. Steve's mom felt that the information given by the nurse wasn't consistent with the story her son had told.

Let's take a closer look at this story. Initially, Steve adjusted to school very quickly and made friends instantly. This is a common sign of involvement in Greek life or other groups that include hazing activities as a part of initiation. In the beginning of the semester, the fraternities and sororities are in competition with one another for new members. They appeal to the new students by offering a sense of security, a place to go, and instant friends. It's hard to resist and many students want and need such an affiliation.

The quickness of the adjustment period, especially for someone like Steve, who had never really spent time away from home, is the first indication that he might have been involved in a fraternity even though he had decided, prior to college, not to join one.

At the same time, Steve changed the pace and pattern of communication with his parents. In the fall semester, he spoke with his mother on a daily basis. Suddenly, he announced a significant change.

He would call once a week and prohibited his mom from calling him at all. This is another indication of fraternity life and the possibility of hazing, as students are often encouraged to reduce contact with people outside the group, including their friends and families. When Steve did speak to his mom, he was irritable and short, in contrast to the first semester, when he was cooperative and interested in communicating.

When Steve's mom received the call at 2:30 A.M., she knew something wasn't right with her son. Even before speaking to the nurse, she felt her son's story didn't make sense. Why go to the hospital after a minor injury to your finger, and why go at 2:30 A.M. on a school night, thirty-six hours after the injury occurred? Though she knew it didn't seem logical, she didn't know what was happening with her son. She had suspected that Steve was involved in pledging, but she didn't know enough about the process to add up the disparate pieces of the puzzle.

The signs and cues that Steve's mom saw were subtle and could have indicated many things. Remember the game, "What's wrong with this picture?" where you'd look at a picture that seemed fine, but when you examined it closely, things were upside down, out of order, or askew? The same thing happens in the early stages of hazing. You may become aware of small details that just don't add up.

This chapter gives you tips on what to look for as signs of hazing involvement. As you read, you'll probably think, "All these things have happened to my kids." Your feeling is correct, which is why it is so very difficult to discern an act of hazing from the regular predicaments that kids end up in. The following discussion will supply you with some questions to ask or paths to investigate, which will help you discover if the signs you are seeing are the result of hazing.

WARNING SIGNS OF HAZING

The warning signs of hazing come in different shapes and forms. Many occur in situations that aren't necessarily due to hazing. This is an important point. My goal is not to scare you into believing your child or student is involved in hazing but to urge you to keep your eyes and ears open to the signs of something being askew. Even if it turns out not to be due to hazing, you'll still be helping your child. Once again, I advise parents, teachers, and coaches to follow their gut. You know your children and students better than anyone else. When something smells fishy and it looks fishy, it probably is fishy and worthy of further investigation.

There are five warning signs that are noticeable when a child is becoming involved in an organization that hazes as part of its initiation. A child may

1. Adjust too quickly to new situations and instantly have new friends
2. Change the pattern of communication
3. Reduce contact with old friends and family
4. Develop new physical and medical problems
5. Develop new psychological problems

Let's take a more detailed look at each warning sign.

Adjusts Too Quickly to New Situations and Has Instant Friends

Instant friends, instant acceptance, and an instant place to hang out are often associated with groups that use initiation rituals. The instantaneousness of the change is what is remarkable. For students such as Steve, who have never been away from home, there is usually a period of homesickness, followed by a slow adjustment phase. The fact that these stages seemed to have been missing with Steve doesn't necessarily reflect a well-adjusted kid. Most new students feel awkward, uncomfortable, or shy, and it usually takes time to find and establish new friendships. Parents' antennae should go up when they hear about an adjustment that seems too smooth, too easy, and too instantaneous.

Perhaps there's one other important factor to consider. You know your child's personality and style. Some kids can walk into a room and find friends easily; most kids can't. If you have an extroverted child whose style enables him to make friends easily, the quick adjustment may be typical and not a sign that he's getting involved in a group that hazes. But if this type of behavior is out of character for your child, keep your eyes and ears open for other possible warning signs.

Changes in Pattern of Communication

Usually, there is a pattern that is established between students and their family regarding when and how to communicate. For students living away from home, it may be *multi-modal*, including telephone calls, e-mails, instant messages, as well as frequent care packages. For others, it may be the once-a-week telephone call. For students living at home, there may be a spontaneous moment or planned event that ensures that the parent and child spend some quality time talking. Whatever the pattern is that you've established, if your child changes it radically, including a change in the frequency, length of time, or tone of the communication, I'd become suspicious of something troubling your child.

For example, Steve and his mom spoke on a daily basis for at least fifteen minutes each call. Steve's mother called him every evening, and he'd call during the day if he needed to. Once pledge season arrived, Steve changed the rules and told his mom not to call him, ever! He also said that he'd call only once a week. Steve did call but usually spoke for one minute. This sudden and extreme change in the pattern and rules of communication is significant.

A radical change in the emotional tone and content of the calls without apparent reason can also be a sign of trouble. Before leaving for college, Steve's emotional tone was lively and he shared his thoughts, feelings, and experiences with his parents and friends. As Steve began the pledge process, he became more distant, more aggressive, and much less talkative. Suddenly, he accused his mom of being too involved and too intrusive. Although this could be true, it was, in fact, a way for Steve to dodge his mom and avoid contact with her. He knew that she would detect something in his voice and would be concerned by his activities.

The radical change in communication is quite noticeable among hazing victims. The various, time-consuming group activities they become involved in make it less likely that they'll have the time or energy to communicate with family or friends. In addition, they often feel uncomfortable about the hazing and avoid contact with those who might detect a change in their emotional state.

Reduces Contact with Family and Friends

Abandoning old friends and family is often a behavior associated with joining a group that demands allegiance. In Steve's case, he severely reduced contact with his parents and completely cut off ties with his friends from home. This reduction in contact and communication with people outside the group serves to establish distinct group boundaries. The group leaders, like the team captain or fraternity president, use this tactic to strengthen their control over the group, intending to replace the role of parents and other authority figures in the lives of the group members.

The group leaders believe that creating an aura of exclusivity will strengthen the group's identity. In other words, people not in the group are considered to be outsiders and not equal in status to the insiders. There is often pressure on those new to the group to reduce or eliminate contact with previous friends who aren't seeking membership in the same group. This solidifies the "us versus them" mentality, implying that "we" are better than "they" are.

Newcomers are the most likely candidates to exhibit this warning sign. As part of the initiation process, the group leaders often act as if they "own" the victim. In fact, sometimes pledge masters and team captains actually call them their *slave* or *bitch*. The expectation is that the victim will only participate in the activities of that group. The leader requires the victim to cut off communication with those outside the group. This is seen most dramatically in fraternities and sororities.

Rise in New Kinds of Physical and Medical Problems

By the time your child enters high school or college, you know the typical kinds of ailments that he is prone to. As with everyone, students seem to have at least one vulnerable organ. Some kids are likely to get colds and bronchitis, whereas others suffer from sensitive stomachs. Regardless of the kind of problem, parents know which are common for their own child. However, there are times when your child is suddenly suffering from symptoms that are unusual for him, such as broken bones, sprains, and bruising. When visits to the emergency room are more frequent than usual or when medical attention seems warranted and is different from your child's usual pattern, consider the possibility that hazing is the cause.

Surprisingly, both victims and perpetrators show the same kind of physical signs when a hazing is occurring. For example, pledges often are sleep deprived and the pledge masters, (those in charge of the pledges), are often in a similar state because they need to be watching the pledges. Other symptoms, such as sore throats, may arise. Pledge masters often scream at pledges for hours, resulting in hoarseness and throat pain. Pledges, on the other hand, may be vomiting from binge drinking or excessive consumption of spicy foods for hours, causing them sore throats. In contrast, bystanders are less likely to show the same physical symptoms as victims and perpetrators, although they may have experienced similar symptoms in the past, when they were new to the group.

Once again, these are common symptoms due to many causes, one of which may be hazing. Symptoms due to hazing are often more frequent and more severe than those caused by typical sources. Some of the symptoms due to hazing are

- *Exhaustion.* Kids become so exhausted that they either admit or sound as if they have not slept in days. They may be incoherent and tell you that they need to sleep. Sleep deprivation is an extremely common form of hazing, particularly in college.

- *Bumps and bruises.* High school hazing frequently results in bumps and bruises that simply do not match the sport. For example, in wrestling the hazing often involves red bellies, which are caused by being hit with a towel until your stomach is red. This kind of irritation is not caused by the usual moves found in wrestling.

- *Cuts and burns.* Scars in unusual places could be an indication of cuts and burns that were done with a purpose. Burning, such as with a cigarette, or branding aren't uncommon in fraternity and sorority hazing. Using a barbecue igniter has occurred in high school hazing.

- *Sore throats and stomachaches.* This is such a common symptom that it will be difficult to determine the cause. However, when the student is completely unable to talk, swallow, or eat, the sore throat may be due to eating excessive amounts of spicy foods or from excessive vomiting. Stomachaches are similar. If the student complains of diarrhea, vomiting, or intense pain, it may be due to the ingestion of large quantities of nonfood items (such as live goldfish, hamsters, mealy worms, dog biscuits) or alcohol or combinations of foods that are intended to cause pain and suffering. Again, it is the intensity or severity of the symptom that indicates a hazing-related injury. These symptoms are common in both high school and college students.

- *Severe headaches.* Dehydration is a prime cause of severe headaches resulting from hazing. In both high school and college, students' excessive consumption of alcohol is likely to cause dehydration. Sometimes excessive amounts of other liquids, including water, milk, or prune juice are used instead of or in addition to alcohol. Subsequent vomiting and diarrhea may occur and dehydration may result from this as well.

Blows to the head, causing concussions, are another cause of severe headaches. In the winter of 2004, a girl on a Florida high school soccer team was dropped on her head while being initiated with a *swirlie* (putting her head in a toilet and flushing it). Days later, when she was suffering from a severe headache, she went to the hospital and was diagnosed with a concussion and subsequent neurological damage.

- *Hospital visits*. Most hazing-related hospital visits are caused by a combination of events, resulting in an accidental or intentional injury. Usually, visits to the emergency room are due to overdoses of alcohol or drugs, which have been ingested in amounts or time periods that are abnormal for that individual, like ten shots of whiskey in ten minutes. Other emergencies may be accident related, requiring various kinds of medical attention. Though medical staffs may suspect hazing as the cause of the injuries, they rarely report it as such.

Develops New Psychological Symptoms

From my point of view, the psychological scars of hazing are far deeper than the physical. There is something about the emotional connections made prior to, during, and after hazing events that

---

> ➤ **DID YOU KNOW** ≪

Dr. Michelle Finkel, an emergency medicine physician from Massachusetts General Hospital, found that students who are hazed typically do not report the true cause of their injuries because they are embarrassed or because they want to protect those who caused the injuries. Dr. Finkel believes that hazing is very underreported because health care providers don't consider hazing as a possible factor, so they don't ask appropriate questions. She believes that an important warning sign is the inconsistency between the patient's explanation and the actual kind of injury sustained.[1]

engrave in one's mind and soul. Time and time again, people tell me with glee and with shame of their hazing experiences. They do not usually focus on the physical traumas but rather on the psychological ones.

Overriding any particular symptom are two emotions: *betrayal* and *disbelief*. Victims and perpetrators often feel betrayed and lose the ability to trust for a long period of time. Bystanders, as well as others, often reflect on their behavior with disbelief, wondering how they allowed themselves to be involved and why they didn't do anything to stop it.

Any kind of involvement in hazing is likely to cause a personality shift. Steve's mother noted this in the example at the beginning of this chapter. Even though Steve and his mom had enjoyed a close and positive relationship, he quickly became distant and snarly. Steve's mom saw a change in him that grew more and more negative as the second semester progressed.

Often it is the psychological changes and symptoms that are most noticeable to family, friends, teachers, and coaches. This is because kids are savvy at hiding the physical signs of hazing. However, they are less able to hide the psychological changes and symptoms. The following list contains some classic signs of psychological problems. All can occur independently and unrelated to hazing. However, as with the physical symptoms, it's the severity and sometimes-sudden onset that you should be attuned to. Anyone who is suffering from such symptoms should seek professional help, regardless of the apparent cause of the problem.

Some typical psychological warning signs are

• *Change in sleeping and eating patterns*. These are the first signs that psychiatrists look for. They are called *vegetative signs*, meaning that they've caused a change in the way that the student's body normally functions. You may notice a significant increase or decrease in weight or a significant change in sleep patterns (increased need for sleep, difficulty getting to sleep, difficulty staying asleep, waking early, not being able to wake up, or having nightmares). This symp-tom is most commonly found among victims; however, in situations where hazardous hazing is occurring, it is possible that bystanders and perpetrators may be suffering from sleep disturbance, due to anxiety produced by the hazing.

• *Fears and worries*. Anxiety is a primary reaction to hazing because the student doesn't know how to deal with the hazing and might be unsure if another hazing is likely to occur. There's a sense of doom and foreboding that you might hear in their voice or in their reluctance to participate in activities. Sometimes the student may not be able or willing to attend classes, practices, or group meetings. Their avoidance of these activities may be an appropri-ate response, because they expect the hazing to continue. Again, when the initiation rites have spun out of control, it is possible that victims, bystanders, and perpetrators will be anxious, fearful, and worried, even though each group is worried for different reasons. Perpetrators are afraid of getting caught; bystanders are afraid of los-ing their season or chapter (the future of the group); and victims are afraid of the hazing that seems to be increasingly dangerous.

• *Irritability*. Often kids want to hide information from their parents, and they become incredibly irritable, cutting off the con-versation as soon as possible. This may be a sign of hazing, especially if the pattern of contact between you and the student has changed significantly and abruptly.

• *Anger and negativity*. Depressive symptoms, in which the stu-dent is more aggressive than usual, or the opposite, where the student is more passive, may indicate that hazing has occurred. A sudden attitude that "everything sucks" and feelings of hopelessness can be symptoms of depression.

A victim might be angry at the perpetrators for their actions and at the bystanders for not stopping the perpetrators. They might also be angry at themselves for being in such a situation. If parents or other relatives had encouraged joining the group that hazes, the vic-tim may be angry at them as well. Likewise, perpetrators, who believe that they have caused significant harm or that they may be reported to outside authorities, may be angry toward those reporting the hazing.

• *Poor concentration.* Inability to concentrate or maintain attention to tasks, especially those that were relatively easy to pay attention to in the past, may be another indication of stress and anxiety. Once again, it is the victim that is most likely to have this symptom, though if an investigation is occurring and bystanders and perpetrators believe that they may be held responsible, psychological problems such as poor concentration may evolve for them too.

• *Drop in achievement.* When kids are stressed, their achievement in school, athletics, and other extracurricular activities suffer. Though many people consider this as part of the normal adjustment to high school or college, it is not necessarily just that. A sudden, precipitous decline may be a possible reaction to hazing events. Likewise, due to their participation in the initiation activities, bystanders and perpetrators may suffer academically, as their time is redirected toward pledge or group activities.

• *Obsessions and compulsions.* Sometimes kids involved in hazing find that images and sounds repeat in their mind and they aren't able to "turn off" the scenes. Repetitive thoughts or actions are a way to deal with overwhelming anxiety and usually warrant some psychological intervention. This symptom is closely associated with victims, who may be extremely upset by their circumstances. However, bystanders and perpetrators might develop these symptoms if they are conflicted by the hazing events, or if they fear they'll be reported.

These brief descriptions of the hazing warning signs will help you be alert to changes in the behavior of your children and students. But sometimes these warning signs are so subtle that they are impossible to see. Because kids are adept at hiding and sliding beneath our parental radar, we must become equally adept at uncovering signs that may be almost invisible. Keeping our eyes and ears open to what others are saying can be extremely fruitful. This technique is something I like to call "listening to the chatter."

LISTENING TO THE CHATTER

Usually, we tell our kids not to listen to those who are whispering, as we consider gossip to be negative and false. Certainly, informal chatter and gossip are frequently incorrect or a gross exaggeration of the facts. However, sometimes the chatter has been built around a shred of truth. I find that in those communities that have experienced hazing, both in high school and college settings, there has often been chatter about the subject or hazing event. Sometimes the chatter is not recognized as hazing or seems too incredible to believe and is dismissed.

An Insider's View of Hazing

As parents, we thought we knew what was best for him, but we misread our son's requests to come home from a preseason football camp. At first, we thought he was suffering from homesickness and encouraged him to stay. He called another time and said he even had a ride back, but we felt that he needed to bond with the rest of the team. We knew there was some kind of initiation because we had heard some rumors, but we trusted the coach. However, when he returned home from camp, he called an uncle and asked if they use brooms during a hazing. This was our first clue that something horrible had happened to our son. The coach never even said he was sorry. We felt betrayed by the coach, the team, and the community.

—MARIA, parent of a high school hazing victim

Whether or not we want to believe the rumor mill, it is often true that listening to the grapevine has some merit. Dismiss that which seems irrelevant. But pay attention when you hear about a teacher, coach, group, or fraternity that engages in questionable practices, cruel or inappropriate punishment, favoritism, or impulsive actions.

When listening to the chatter, take a moment to evaluate the information that seems troubling. Bad reputations don't usually survive unless the behaviors have been repeatedly evident. Before your child joins teams, clubs, or Greek organizations, spend some time checking out the informal information. Even before your child goes to high school or college, become acquainted with the various organizations that he is interested in. At orientation, both you and your student should ask around and learn as much as possible about the groups, their leaders, and the "real deal."

Teachers and coaches also need to take the chatter seriously. You are sometimes in a better position than the parents are to investigate the truth. If you hear about hazing activities at your school, consider them to be true to some extent until you have proven to yourself that they're false. It is better to err on the side of being too cautious. It is also possible that students want you to hear about the hazing in hopes that you'll intervene or stop it.

My research has indicated that 75 percent of the time, people believe that the coaches or authority figures do in fact know about the hazing rituals. When coaches and athletic directors were questioned, 50 percent knew there had been hazing in their communities. Frequently, hazing accounts include descriptions of a coach walking into, encouraging, or participating in hazing. In New Mexico, in 2005, six eighth graders were drafted onto the high school basketball team. On the way back home from the first "away" game, the new members were seated in the front of the bus, behind the coaches. The athletic director told them to go to the back of the bus, where the older members of the team hazed them. The victims were kicked, punched, and thrown so that they hit the ceiling of the bus. One student was hospitalized with damage to his back and spleen.

Whether you're a parent, teacher, or coach, the information you gather informally, by paying attention to the chatter, may help you discover hazing. Sometimes the information helps you assemble the pieces of the puzzle so that the big picture suddenly comes into focus.

Here are some thoughts to consider as you plug into the chatter in your community or campus:

1. What kinds of hazing activities are being mentioned?
2. When does the hazing occur? (day, night, or season)
3. Is the hazing related to a specific group? If so, which one?
4. Is there a specific person or group leading the hazing? If so, who?
5. Are there specific locations associated with the hazing? If so, where?
6. How long has the chatter been circulating through the community?
7. Have any authorities ever investigated the chatter?
8. How frequently have you heard the same accusations?
9. What is the emotional tenor of the chatter? Does it feel accurate?

Err on the side of caution. Take the chatter seriously. Investigate. Trust your gut.

APPROACHING A HAZING PARTICIPANT

You have enough information to suspect that a hazing has occurred. You know that there's a group that may have been involved in a hazing, but you don't know who may have been victimized, who may have been the perpetrators, and who may have watched.

Now What?

There's no easy answer. It's likely that you'll hit a wall of silence about the possible hazing incident. Part of hazing behavior is train-ing all those involved, including the victims, to use the same cover story in case anyone outside of the group becomes suspicious. In addition, the victims and bystanders have often been intimidated and threatened, so they are wary of breaking the code of silence. (This is discussed in greater detail in the next chapter.)

The most important communication at this time is to assure your child or student that you'll be on his side, to support and help him through the crisis. You need to repeatedly tell him that you'll take care of him and find a way to work through the problem. *Pro-tecting the trusting relationship needs to be your first priority.*

Remember that your child or student has been traumatized and may not trust anyone, not even a parent or sibling, and therefore you must be patient and available. Though this is especially true for the victims, it also holds true for bystanders and perpetrators. Regardless of their role, adolescents are traumatized by the events even if they're acting callous and nonchalant. Interpret this bravado as a way to mask their anxiety.

Direct questioning of suspected participants will probably lead to direct denial. So more subtle approaches should be used. It all goes back to building trust and engaging in informal conversations. I believe that kids often *want to tell* what has happened to them or to others, particularly if it is upsetting to them. Though they may adhere to the unspoken oath (what goes on in the locker room stays in the locker room and other variations on this theme), I believe that they'd be relieved to tell a trusted person about their secret, the hazing.

Approach all kids in a low-key manner. Consider yourself a reporter who needs to protect your source of information, while simultaneously needing to get the story. Promise confidentiality, something that you must do, if you intend to maintain trust with that student. Remember, at this point, your main goal is not to get a kid in trouble. Punishment, consequences, and legal issues aren't paramount at this time.

Your main goal is gathering additional information, protecting students from physical or psychological harm, and stopping hazing activities from occurring again.

The First Thirty-Six Hours

There is a *critical time frame* that exists, in which victims are ready to tell what has occurred during a hazing. This is within thirty-six hours of the actual hazing, especially when the victims have been seriously betrayed. The physical wounds often prompt the victims to seek medical attention. It is at this point that the medical staff needs to question the "cover stories," because oftentimes they know that the explanation doesn't match the injury. But the victims are also psychologically traumatized, and often in shock. They can't believe that those they trusted could hurt and humiliate them to such a degree.

It is during this period of shock that the trauma unpins the student, and he's so stunned that he has a deep need to report what has happened. He knew that things might happen but never expected the activities to become so aggressive, so sexual, so humiliating, and he especially didn't expect to be the victim of the abuse—abuse perpetrated by those who are considered "brothers" or "teammates," people that he was taught to trust implicitly. The stark reality that these very people purposely betrayed him is too much to take, and the victim is furious. At this point, his rage needs to be expressed, and it's at this point, when the victim is somewhat out of control, somewhat traumatized, and extremely emotionally overwhelmed, that he is likely to tell the truth.

The time frame is short, and after about thirty-six hours, the victims will start to repress their feelings. As the physical wounds start to heal, as the student starts to feel "normal" again, his rationality returns and his emotions are checked. Psychologically, it is as though the scab that is covering the cuts is also covering the psychic wounds.

The victim realizes that his choices are limited. If he chooses to report the events, all members of the group may ostracize him. At a fraternity, he'll likely be referred to as a *dead pledge*, and in addition, they'll treat him with less respect and may even threaten and intimidate him. These kinds of groups make it seem that the secrets they have shared are sacred, and if you reveal any of them, you're sinning.

In addition, the perpetrators will reinforce the rhetoric of the group, reminding the victim that this has been passed on for generations and that he is stronger and better for having survived the various head games and physical feats. The victims will frequently succumb, either because they are afraid to oppose the group or because of their great need to belong to the group, despite their pain and suffering. For some, the need for affiliation and acceptance overcomes their core values. There are other victims who simply leave the campus, the team, or the group, due to their trauma or due to the belief that their life will be hell.

After the First Thirty-Six Hours

It is the victim who is most likely to "spill the beans" within the first thirty-six hours of having been humiliated and betrayed. Bystanders and perpetrators may begin to brag about the events, days, weeks, and months after a hazing. Frequently, the bystanders and perpetrators believe that the hazing is funny. This is partially because they also have been hazed, and they need to rationalize the process. Hazing others also serves to make the person feel whole again, by regaining his sense of self-worth and strength. It is as though they need to haze others in order to recoup themselves.

Part of this process seems to include telling others about the adventures, and since the advent of cell phones with cameras, evidence is often captured. Sometimes the humiliating photos are posted on the Internet. As a parent, teacher, or coach, you might find out about hazing in a variety of ways and at varying intervals. The important thing to remember is that any information is significant, as it is likely that another hazing will occur in a similar way and at the same place in the future.

Questions to Ask

If you interact with anyone you suspect was involved in a hazing, the following topics and questions are a great starting point to your discussion:

1. Safety First
   - Are you hurt? If so, tell me every body part that is or was in pain.
   - Are you sleeping well? If not, how is your sleep disturbed?
   - Are you eating as usual? If not, how has it changed?
   - Are you afraid of anything? If so, what?

2. What Happened?
   - "I know something has happened. I can feel that you are different. Please tell me. I promise I will keep everything confidential, but I must know what happened."
   - When did these events occur?
   - How did this happen?

3. Information
   - Who else knows about this?
   - Who else did this happen to?
   - Has this happened before?
   - Has this been reported?
   - What is your role in this?

Parenting, teaching, and coaching have become more challenging in the past ten years. Now every adult has to be part parent, part detective, and part doctor, while maintaining all the other aspects of life. I hope that this chapter sensitized you to some of the subtle cues and clues your child or student may be exhibiting. Becoming more aware of these warning signs, whether hazing related or not, is crucial to help our children and students get through their adolescence safely and enjoyably.

4

Helping a Victim of Hazing

In the spring of 2005, Zach was a fifteen-year-old freshman beginning his high school career as a member of the school's football team in a small town in Kentucky. The spring football hazing began when an upperclassman took a wooden pole, used to move the stage curtain, and rammed it into Zach's groin area twice. The next day, the same boy slapped Zach in the groin area. The following day, the hazing continued, with the upperclassmen throwing water bottles and footballs at the groin area of the freshmen, treating them as servants, and referring to them as bitches. *Zach and his peers tried to defend themselves. The coaches just laughed and did nothing. At football practice, Zach was hit in the head with a football helmet, and a bump larger than a grapefruit appeared immediately. The head football coach didn't call Zach's parents, nor did he seek medical attention for Zach's injury.*

With school officials not admitting to any hazing problems, and the community not willing to support people who report such incidents to the police or the media, Zach's parents were unsure of how to help their son. They decided to formally report the hazing and file charges against the school administration and school board because they had not received appropriate responses from any of the officials that they contacted.

Months later, three more students were discovered hitting underclassmen in the groin area. This came much to the community's surprise, because school officials had claimed that Zach's case was an isolated incident. The local newspaper continues to report about similar hazing problems found in the local school system.

How can you help when a victim is ready to report a hazing incident? There are many steps to be taken, choices to be made, and questions to be answered, such as when and where to file the report, how it should be filed, and what is needed. However, before you even think about reporting a hazing, you must be ready to actually break the code of silence and tell the story of the hazing to the world. It's a much tougher choice than you may realize.

The dilemma about what to do weighs heavily on everyone's shoulders—parents, students, and even me. As I approached this chapter, I received e-mails from mothers of high school kids who had been hazed during the previous school year. These parents reported the hazing and were frantic, worrying about repercussions that might continue as their kids returned to school after the summer vacation. All of these families are suffering so much. How could I suggest that telling is better than not telling?

I spoke with Karen Savoy, founder of Mothers Against School Hazing (MASH). As I described in Chapter Two, Karen and her husband, Jerry, strongly supported their son, Jake, who reported a brutal hazing. I explained my situation and Karen responded quickly and firmly. "I've got my pride. There is not one thing I would do differently. Exposing the hazing allowed me and my son to regain our pride. This has been a very difficult road; however, I could not have chosen a different path. Because of Jake's strength, others have come forth. I can sleep at night because I know that I protected my son and other people's sons; I can hold my head high, because we have done the right thing. I have my pride."

Zach's mom also felt that coming forward and reporting the incident was beneficial, because other kids started to come forward and report the same exact kinds of behaviors. This meant that it was the bravery of her son, and her family, that opened the door for others.

Breaking the code of silence, standing up for what you think is right, and questioning authority figures are things that anyone can choose to do. Often we don't do any of these things because we're able to tolerate whatever has happened. But when it's your son or daughter who's been hazed, or when it's your job that will be lost, your impetus to report hazing is increased. Regardless of your reason, reporting a hazing is a courageous thing to do.

HOW TO BREAK THE CODE OF SILENCE

The code of silence is an unwritten understanding among any group of people not to tell if something happens that may be illegal, immoral, or unethical. Sometimes the code of silence is a natural reaction to a trauma and sometimes intimidation is used to reinforce the code. At its best, the code of silence protects, and at its worst, it causes pain and suffering, allowing destructive situations to continue.

The power behind the code of silence is based on fear, and this fear makes us not want to break the silence. We are scared to expose our family or our group to a situation that might involve further pain, suffering, or humiliation or possible legal ramifications. Sometimes the fear is real and intimidation and threats are used. Sometimes the fear is implied, such as the fear of retribution or social isolation.

The central issue in breaking the code of silence is overcoming your fear and making the choice to create change. If you choose to tell about the events that you know have occurred, suspect have occurred, or believe will occur, you're being proactive and brave. Making this choice to tell is extremely difficult. However, in the following sections, I have provided some questions that I hope will aid you in your decision.

> ➤ **DID YOU KNOW** ◄

Surveys of high school and college students indicate that many would not break the code of silence and report a hazing under any circumstance. Ninety-five percent of high school students would not report a hazing, and 44 percent of fraternity and sorority members would not report.[1] In addition, 60 percent of college athletes would not report a hazing.[2]

Families

Families face tremendous pressure when trying to decide whether or not to report a hazing incident. Often fathers are most concerned about the reaction of the community. The implication about their own child's reputation and the possibility of hostility and revenge lead fathers to fear that their entire family will be harmed. In contrast, mothers are often bursting with rage. They feel betrayed by the authority figure, who did not adequately protect their child. This split creates more tension within the family because the parents do not agree about the best course of action. Add to this the victim's own fears about how he'll fit in after telling, and the scene is set for an emotional meltdown.

Sometimes students are the bravest of us all. They may feel very sure that the truth must be told and the suffering must be exposed. Other times, the students are less clear and feel more allegiance to their peer group or more hesitation about the best course of action. To help parents and kids decide whether to break the code of silence, I suggest you consider the following questions:

1. If I do report this hazing, what is the best thing that may happen now or in the future? What is the worst?

2. If I do not report this hazing, what will happen in the future?

- What may happen to my son or daughter, my other children, or my family?

- What may happen to other students?

3. Parents should consider this: What *life lessons* am I teaching my children by my decision?

4. Parents should also consider this: What kind of role model am I being for my kids?

Teachers, Coaches, Supervisors

Teachers, coaches, supervisors, psychologists, and other professionals are often directed by legal or ethical obligations, and their choices about whether or not to report hazing is less difficult than it is for parents. However, before anyone follows rules, she has to make an individual choice that may seem to involve risk.

For example, all mandated *reporters* (professionals who work with children) must report any suspicion of child abuse. However, before they make the call to the child abuse hot line, they often consider their options. Once a report is made, a long string of actions occurs, many of which may directly involve the mandated reporter. Reporters may choose to diminish the severity of the child abuse (in their own mind) as a way to rationalize not making the report. This same kind of dilemma exists with hazing. Many teachers, coaches, and supervisors diminish the acts of hazing as a way of not getting involved.

Legally, there are several sets of rules and laws that each professional working with children needs to be informed about. State law takes precedence over all other rules and regulations, such as school district policy, and over the requirements of an organization, such as a club sport, church group, or fraternity or sorority. However, all of these organizations should also have a clearly defined hazing policy, along with details of how the policy is enforced.

Communicating the state and local laws, as well as the hazing policy, is part of the proper training of the individual who's responsible for the group of students. Hazing prevention training should

An Insider's View of Hazing

My son was a freshman at a southern college and the pledging began by being forced to eat so many raw onions and other spicy foods that he had burns of his mouth, throat, and esophagus severe enough to keep him from eating or drinking for more than twenty-four hours. My husband, a physician, went to see him and found him to be dehydrated and in excruciating pain. However, my son refused to go to health services or report the abuse. The frat boys continued to pester him day and night with absurd, meaningless tasks that demanded his time, with no regard for academics. For example, during a thirty-six-hour scavenger hunt, items on the list were given different point values. The highest number of points was accorded to "a vial of crack cocaine." Later in the semester, at the Big Brother Night, each pledge was subjected to funneling (having large quantities of unidentified alcohol poured down the throat) and then hot sauce poured on his genitals and anus. As you can imagine, we wanted him to quit the fraternity, but he refused to de-pledge, claiming that he had invested so much energy and that de-pledging might have serious consequences.

Interestingly, he learned a few things about the myth of "brotherhood." In situations where he expected his fraternity brothers to stand up for him, they didn't. This is a life lesson I'm sure he'll never forget. These events have also created a closer relationship between our son, my husband, and myself. Our son promises to report everything to us and to refuse to do anything that will cause him medical harm.

—PAULA, mother of a freshman pledge in a National fraternity occur on a regular basis, and it's the responsibility of the governing body to provide such education. In addition, it's in the best interests of the coaches, teachers, or supervisors to be informed about the current hazing policy and to know what their individual legal responsibility is if they have information about a hazing. For further resources on hazing laws in your state, see the Resource Guide at the back of this book.

Ethically, professionals need to decide whether they should report the information about a hazing event. Though it may seem like an easy decision when read in a book, reality is quite different. To begin with, as a professional, you may not be sure how accurate your information is. You may feel that the hazing is unrelated to you as it involves kids or adults who aren't in your class, team, or school. You may feel that the hazing ritual is a long-standing tradition that is essentially harmless. You may feel that all this hazing stuff is just more "politically correct" rhetoric. You may be scared to report hazing because a close friend or colleague, or you yourself, might get into trouble. All these conflicts, and others, may cloud your decision.

Every time a hazing occurs, everyone involved is likely to repeat the behavior, increasing the number and severity of hazings. Conversely, every time a hazing is stopped, the chain is broken, decreasing the likelihood that hazing will be done by those students again. In fact, students who have been stopped from hazing often become leaders in the fight against hazing. Hank Nuwer, an author who has been writing about hazing for more than twenty-eight years, began to uncover hazing because of his own experience as a bystander.

Another reason to stop hazing is that anyone—teachers, coaches, or supervisors—may be held legally responsible for hazing. As the laws become more forceful, more and more coaches and teachers are being held responsible. Therefore your job, your reputation, and your future may be influenced if your students haze.

Of course, the most compelling reason to report a hazing is to keep students from being harmed. We never know when people are suffering physically or psychologically nor the degree to which their life is in danger. In February 2005, Donna, Texas, was shocked by a hazing on its high school football team. Eight underclassmen were hazed and sexually assaulted by four upperclassmen, who held victims down while placing a latex-gloved finger into the boys' anuses. Similar incidents occurred involving hitting of buttocks and genitals. The Texas Education Agency reported that hazing incidents had been occurring for several years, and coaches knew of these events and tolerated sexual assaults in the men's locker room.[3]

If you're still ambivalent about whether to report information related to hazing, consider what happens to you, the students, and the community if you choose not to report:

1. What happens if a student is seriously injured during a hazing?

2. What kind of role model are you for your students if you allow hazing to occur, overtly or covertly?

3. What message are you sending to all your students—potential victims, bystanders, and perpetrators—if you don't report the hazing?

4. What happens to you, your class, or your team if a higher authority discovers the hazing events and you did not report them?

5. What is the worst-case scenario if a hazing occurs, and you have not created or followed a policy intended to prevent hazing?

6. How will you feel when you have to tell a parent that her child was seriously harmed due to a hazing incident?

7. How does hazing affect your reputation?

8. Will parents lose trust in you if hazing occurs in your group?

9. Why would you want to allow hazing to continue?

Fraternity and Sorority Leaders

Fraternities and sororities are facing difficult times. Besides decreasing enrollment and increasing insurance costs, the legal and policy changes regarding initiation rites are becoming more stringent each day. When the National Greek organizations or the colleges suspend a chapter, they are doing their best to limit dangerous behaviors. However, this does not always stop the hazing behavior. Often the members of a suspended chapter will simply move across the street and invent a new, rogue, fraternity that will continue to act in dangerous ways. These groups reflect badly on everyone: on the original recognized Greek affiliate, on the school, and on the community. Once the students become unrecognized, unaffiliated, suspended, or rogue, no one is in control.

Another issue that faces fraternity and sorority leaders is that the organizations differ regionally. National Greek organizations have the daunting task of trying to maintain certain standards. The National organizations try to control all the chapters across the country by instilling specific rules and regulations. However, each chapter has its own local traditions, and each college has different rules that might influence the behaviors of the members.

Just like coaches who have an incredible amount of power with athletes, the leaders of Greek organizations also have tremendous power to influence the actions of their members. That means that each and every Greek officer, member, and alumnus should feel personally responsible for the physical and emotional well-being of their brothers and sisters. They need to know that there are real consequences for hazing activities.

If you're a Greek leader or member and you're ambivalent about reporting a hazing, please consider the following questions:

1. What's the worst-case scenario of not reporting hazing?

2. What are my personal responsibilities if a pledge is seriously hurt during an initiation? What if I could have prevented or

intervened? What if I didn't report it and now the pledge has died? How will that affect the rest of my life?

3. What are the consequences to the National and local chapter of the fraternity or sorority if a hazing occurs and was not reported?

4. What are the consequences to the college if a hazing occurs?

Breaking the code of silence is something that will happen slowly and only if individuals are forced to take responsibility for their part in the hazing. For parents, teachers, coaches, and leaders, that means understanding our responsibility to help the victims and using our power to create and foster change.

REPORTING A HAZING

Once you decide to break the code of silence and tell about a hazing, you may be faced with concrete questions, such as whom do I report it to, how should it be reported, what information do I need to report, what kinds of records should I keep for myself?

Because there are so many variables and state laws and school policies widely differ, it's impossible to give you specifics that relate to your circumstance. But the following general information should help you begin to wade through the maze.

Reporting the Hazing

You have just discovered that your son or daughter was hazed. Whom do you report the incident to? That is a really good question, especially as there are no federal or local agencies that track such reports. Unlike the case with child abuse, there's no general hot line and no one geared to handle hazing. Now what?

Who Should You Report To?

Begin to report the hazing event by contacting the agency that is responsible for the student at the time of the hazing. For example, a student hazed during high school football practice should notify the coach, the principal, and the superintendent of the school district.

In a college, you and your child may choose to notify the coach, if it's athletics related, the Dean of Students, or the National office of the fraternity, if it's pledging related. However, I would also advise you to consider contacting campus security, sometimes called campus police. They are responsible for enforcing laws and codes on most college campuses. If it's necessary, they will advise you to call the town police or another agency.

Some parents of college-aged students have chosen to make anonymous reports of Greek hazing incidents by calling the Student Life coordinator and then speaking with the person in charge of Greek affairs. This is a good starting place, especially if you're concerned but not aware of any serious infractions. In some hazing cases, parents have gone directly to the president of the university. Parents need to consider their options depending on the specific needs of their child and the events that occurred.

When Should Reports Occur?

Report the hazing as soon as possible, regardless of the day or time. Students may be in physical or psychological danger, and of course, these needs must be established and taken care of immediately. Once the victims are stabilized, the hazing should be reported, or if the victim is seeing a doctor or psychologist, the truth should be told to the professionals. In general, the sooner a hazing is reported, the less likely it is to escalate and the fewer people are likely to be seriously harmed.

What Should Be Reported?

Report the truth, the whole truth, and nothing but the truth in as much detail as possible. Information should include location, date, time, names of those present, and the actual events, in chronological order. Damages, physical and psychological, should also be reported. Indicate if further help is needed.

What Happens When a Report Is Made?

After a hazing is reported, there should be a chain of command leading to an official investigation. For example, in Jake Savoy's case from Chapter Two, Jake told his coach, who then called the school principal. An investigation began shortly thereafter. In college, when parents report a suspected hazing, it is investigated by the office of Student Judicial Services or campus police.

At this point, depending on the severity of the hazing, two things can occur. The officials may take it seriously, as they did in the 2001 case of the University of Miami student and fraternity pledge Chad Meredith. After a night of drinking, Chad and two members of his fraternity went swimming in Lake Osceola. Chad, unable to stay afloat, screamed for help before he drowned in seven feet of water, just thirty-four feet from the edge of the lake. His fraternity brothers ignored his pleas and didn't try to save him. This case, along with two previous hazing incidents, led Governor Jeb Bush to sign the toughest hazing law in the nation. The Chad Meredith Act makes hazing that results in significant injury or death a felony in Florida.[4]

In contrast, officials may not take the complaint seriously, as occurred in Zach's case, discussed at the beginning of this chapter. Remember, the office investigating does not necessarily have the same impetus or interest that you have in resolving the hazing. This means that you may have to push each department to explore the issue, eventually spearheading a campaign for justice.

What to Do After Reporting?

After you report a hazing, make sure that you have the name and rank of the person you're reporting to and ask the following questions:

1. What happens next?

2. Who is my contact person?

3. Outline the order of events, now that I have reported the hazing.

4. What is the time line for the investigation?

5. Is there anything else that I should do?

Finally, remember to request a copy of the report for your records.

What Should You Expect Emotionally After Reporting?

Emotionally, you and your child may feel stressed, anxious, and agitated. It's best if you can be with people whom you can trust and who are supportive and caring. In addition, you should be in a safe place, and have a phone available, so that you can be easily contacted. A college student may feel more comfortable at home or off campus.

Everyone will be very vulnerable, sensitive, and edgy after dealing with the shock of a hazing. I have found that the victims and their families feel betrayed, which makes them less trusting toward new people, even those in the helping professions. It's important to realize that everyone may still be in shock, which will be followed by rage and other intense emotions. Creating a comfortable nest, with layers of supportive people, will aid the healing process.

Gathering Information and Keeping Records

Reporting a hazing incident will involve speaking with many different individuals and agencies, and it will help to keep your own records of the process. You can keep your information on a computer, although you might want to print out a copy of all your information as a backup, or send a copy to someone you trust. Even if you're not sure about reporting the event, it's better to have the information than not to have it. Remember, psychological symptoms may arise six months after an event.

Create a file that explains all the information that you and your child know about the hazing event. Include as much detail as possible, including the date and time, the location, and the people involved. This should be done by anyone who's involved, including parents, teachers, coaches, and supervisors. Regardless of the official copy that may be required by the police, hospital, or school, keep your own version.

Please consider doing these things, even if you're not in the mood or don't think you have the time. Details, which seem to be seared in your brain, often fade over time. This information may be relevant later. In addition, writing about the trauma can help you and your child work through it emotionally. It allows you to feel somewhat in control, and it helps you see which questions still need to be answered.

At a minimum, the following items should go in your file:

• An *adult's journal*. Parents, teachers, and coaches should keep a journal, which includes all the information you know. As new events occur, add to your journal, and include not only what happened but also your emotional reactions to the events.

• A *student's journal*. Ask the student to keep a journal, which should include the events that happened in chronological order. Include as much specific information as you can, such as locations, names, details of the hazing activities, and any other relevant information. Your child should write whatever he knows and not worry about remembering every last detail. Tell the student that no one cares about grammar and spelling. They care about the truth and how the student is feeling about himself, his family, his friends, his school, his team, and his future.

A student may be too embarrassed to write about everything that occurred during the hazing, especially the physical and sexual details. However, it's important that the journal contain all details and emotions, no matter how embarrassing they may be. This may be tough to get through to your child, but you must. The truth is your best ally. Reassure your child that the hazing was not his fault and that the journal is a positive way to deal with some of his powerful emotions.

As events continue, have the student add to the journal, including the date and time of the entry and of the events.

• *A telephone and e-mail log.* A log should be kept to record information about each call or e-mail made to relevant individuals and agencies. Include the name of the person, the agency, the date and time, the phone number, the e-mail address, and a summary of the conversation. If possible, send an e-mail thanking them for the call and restating the gist of the conversation, including any specifics about actions that they promised to take. Remember to save all e-mails. In addition, log and print out all instant messages that you or your kids send or receive, regarding the hazing.

• *Visual documentation.* Visual items such as still photos or videotapes are very important. These visuals should illustrate any physical harm that is evident after the hazing. In some cases, actual videotapes or photos (sometimes transmitted via cell phones or e-mail) may be available of the actual hazing. Date the photos or video clips. If there is news footage about the incident, tape that as well. The more proof you have that illustrates the hazing event, the better off you are.

• *Medical records.* All students, regardless of the physical nature of the event, should be seen by a doctor. This is very important. It's always helpful to have a medical professional assess the child, especially if it's someone who knows him and will be able to detect changes in his demeanor and personality. If it's suggested that your child see a specialist, do so immediately. Hospitals in college towns are savvy and can determine if the supposed cause of a trauma matches the cover story given by the students. This may or may not be noted in the medical chart, but you can ask that question to those treating your child.

Ask for copies of all medical information for your own records. There may be a small fee, but the patient is entitled to any and all records. It's easiest to gather the copies at the time of the visit, even though all this information is available to you at a later date. From my own experience I have learned that it's always good to have your own file in case things get lost, misplaced, or mislabeled.

- *Psychological records.* I believe that the true trauma in hazing is the psychological scar that it leaves on everyone involved. I recommend that victims, as well as those family members who have been affected, should be seen by a mental health professional. Record the name and location of the counselor, as well as a summary of the advice given or the actions taken.

Often the counselors or psychologists dismiss the victims from therapy after a few sessions. The parents are told that the kids are fine, even though the parent continues to witness social, academic, or other kinds of problems. If your counselor dismisses your child and you feel that problems continue to exist, consider seeking a second opinion from another kind of specialist, such as a psychiatrist or psychologist. If you do so, try someone in a location that is outside your immediate area, in order to assure yourself that the doctor has not been affected by any local events.

Keep track of all these contacts, bills, and reports. After speaking to any professional, write an entry in your own journal about what your concerns were and what the professional advised.

SHOULD YOU HIRE A LAWYER?

Hazing, especially hazardous hazing, causes physical pain and mental anguish. This often means that lawyers may get involved in order to protect the victim and establish justice. Washington, D.C., attorney Douglas Fierberg (www.hazinglaw.com), an expert in cases involving hazing and other issues of school violence, offers the following guidance:

- *When should an attorney be contacted?* An attorney should be contacted under several conditions. If someone required medical or psychological care, visited the emergency room, or his or her life was endangered, it's likely that a lawsuit should be considered. Before an individual has contact with the media and before any public statements are made, it's helpful to contact an attorney. Organizations such as school districts, colleges, fraternities and sororities, immediately contact their own legal counsel, whom they have retained for crises such as these. Inasmuch as these groups are being advised, it's beneficial for the victims and others to also have legal counsel. As a mother, I would seek legal advice immediately, because a good lawyer can lend information, personal advice, and support, based on experience and knowledge of the law and the media.

• *Where can I find a lawyer?* If you're in a small village, town, or parish, consider going to the largest town or city that's convenient to you. Sometimes it's best if there's some physical distance between the attorney who is representing you and the institutions that may have their own local representation. Regardless of where you live, choose an attorney that is appropriately trained, easily accessible, and someone you feel secure speaking with.

• *What kind of lawyer do I need?* You're looking for either a trial lawyer or a personal injury specialist. Consider consulting the Trial Lawyers of America to find someone well qualified in your area, or contact lawyers who specialize in hazing.

• *Is there specific experience the lawyer needs?* It's helpful if the attorney has had experience in litigating against municipalities or students and has worked on cases that involved school injury. An attorney who has experience with other hazing cases is the best choice.

• *Are retainers required?* Retainers aren't required when hazing cases have involved some kind of damage to the victim. Attorneys almost always take these cases on a contingency basis, meaning that if they win, they get a percentage of the award. The percentage that is given to the lawyer is agreed upon in advance and may either follow state practice or be negotiated. Typical amounts are between 33 percent and 50 percent of the final award.

• *What should the plaintiffs expect (in terms of procedure, time frame, involvement)?* You should expect the attorney to be available to you. The law firm needs to be responsive even at the early stages, in handling publicity, and in directing you toward appropriate kinds of support. The lawyers need to be willing and able to provide time and resources in order to properly handle your case.

Of course, there are many other legal issues to be considered. For additional information on these and other legal issues, please contact a lawyer in your area. See the Resource Guide at the back of the book for additional contacts and Web sites.

DEALING WITH THE MEDIA

The media can provide a way to enlighten the public about the dangers of hazing. But they can also tell a lurid story that is often exaggerated, biased, or unfeeling.

The mass media have become more sensitive to hazing over the last several years and are beginning to report cases more frequently. If the media discover your hazing incident, they may descend upon you and your community as happened in Mepham, New York (described in Chapter One). There, television, radio, and newspaper reporters camped out on the school grounds and swarmed the local bars and pizza parlors. How much media attention the case gets depends on the severity of the events, how available you are for interviews, and the current focus of the specific news organization.

In hazing cases, the media can work for you. Several families who tried to report a hazing had met with resistance until they mentioned the magical "M" word. School districts, colleges, churches, and individuals do not want bad publicity and they respond rapidly when the media may get a whiff of the case. You may choose to report the events to your town or county newspaper, your local television or radio station, or even a national news organization. But please remember, the media are not your friend. They have their own agenda to report news, to make the story intriguing, and sometimes to invade your privacy. So be careful what you wish for and think about what you really hope to gain by going to a media outlet.

Karen Savoy learned how to have the media work for her cause, which was to publicize hazing in high school and the need for better laws. Karen and her son, Jake, appeared on *Oprah*, in *Newsweek*, and in several other newspapers and magazines. Other parents have wanted to shield their children from exposure and publicity and have tried to keep the media away. You must choose what is best for you and your family. To do this, discuss the issue with everyone, especially the victim, because everything about him and his life, and even yours, may become public knowledge.

When dealing with the media, remember the following:

- Speak to your counsel before making any statements to the press.

- Consider appointing a spokesperson to help handle much of the contact with the media.

- Consider whether you want to protect the identity of the victim, especially if the child is young.

- Pick the program, newscaster, or host that you want to speak with by doing research on the program prior to saying yes.

- Ask how the interview will be used.

- Prepare your thoughts in advance and have notes.

- Tell the interviewers any topics that you don't want to discuss before you begin.

- Ask the interviewer, off the record and before the interview begins, what his or her views on hazing are. This will give you an idea of what to expect from the interview.

- Most important, consider your goals, including what's in the best interest of your child.

Breaking the code of silence and reporting a hazing are emotionally charged processes that take strength and courage. Each person has to make his or her own decision about whether or not to file a report. There are many issues to consider. Although it may be the most difficult thing you and your child will ever do, for those who do report, most feel pride. Reporting a hazing is essential to protecting your own rights and the rights of the victim. You have the power to create the change. I hope you choose to use it.

5

Understanding Perpetrators

Chi Tau fraternity pledging at Chico State University in California had begun with simple kinds of tasks, like trading clothing with a homeless person. It was to end with inspiration week, also known as hell week, which included sleeping in a basement so cold that you could see your breath. January 30, 2005, the day that hell week began, was marked by the sewer line breaking, flooding the basement with three inches of sewage-contaminated water. The pledges slept in the basement and were forced to do push-ups and sit-ups in the cold, dank, and toxic conditions. February 1 was called "movie night." While the fraternity pledge general and others played poker and watched a movie, the pledges, wearing only jeans, a T-shirt, and socks, were required to stand on one foot on a wooden bench. They were asked difficult questions, and if they answered wrong, they were told to drink water from a five-gallon bottle or do push-ups on the basement floor. They were also told to douse themselves with the water as fans blew on them to make the experience colder. They had to ask permission to urinate on themselves.

After hours of drinking water and performing calisthenics, Matthew Carrington, a twenty-one-year-old pledge, collapsed and had a seizure for thirty to sixty seconds. A fraternity member began calling 9-1-1 but was told to stop because

*Matthew began to snore. They didn't realize that he was
actually gasping for air. Matthew died on February 2, 2005,
from cardiac dysrhythmia, cerebral edema, and hypothermia
caused by water intoxication.*

One of the fraternity brothers charged with hazing had been the
victim in a similar hazing the previous year. In October 2005,
the four perpetrators pled guilty, thereby avoiding a criminal trial.
The charges ranged from hazing to involuntary manslaughter. The
four perpetrators will spend from ninety days to one year in jail followed by years of probation.[1]

As the parent of a perpetrator who has been involved in a hazing
such as this, you are faced with events that may be startling or may
be all too familiar. Your reaction may be one of disgust and extreme
anger at having your child jeopardize his own life, your life, and the
lives of victims. On the other hand, you may feel that the charges
are unjust and that the hazing is simply an accident or a part of the
culture, a way of life. This chapter will detail the choices and
options that are available as well as the psychological consequences
of being a perpetrator in a hazardous hazing.

UNDERSTANDING THE PERPETRATOR

It may be difficult to imagine how your child would be involved
in something that causes not only humiliation and degradation,
not only cuts and bruises, but also actual death. Certainly, no
one intends to hurt or kill! However, hazardous hazing occurs almost
every week across the United States, and many do involve major
injuries and sometimes death. From 2000 to 2005, more than 120
hazing events occurred that resulted in physical or sexual injury and
at least 27 resulted in deaths of college students.[2,3] Of course, these
statistics don't include the many hazing incidents that go unreported.

It's very, very important to realize that not all perpetrators are "bad
kids." Although some perpetrators do have a history of impulsive,

aggressive, or acting-out behaviors, many don't. Perpetrators are often team captains and leaders. They're often popular, academically successful, and frequently known as "good kids." These are the types of kids other students, parents, teachers, and coaches view as role models.

You may wonder how students, even those that are aggressive and impulsive, can engage in many of the acts recounted in this book. It's important for all of us to understand that often the perpetrators were actually victims during a previous hazing. Their experience as victims primes them to be perpetrators when they finally obtain power and prestige in the group. They are also victims of the tradition. They bought into the group's initiation rite—they "took it"—and now they've followed the rules by reinforcing the hierarchy, demonstrating who has power and control.

Regardless of whether a student has a history of behavioral difficulties, has been a stellar, well-behaved student, or has been a victim of a previous hazing, each perpetrator is responsible for his own actions. Let me be clear about this. Many hazings leave victims scarred either physically, psychologically, or both. The kids who humiliate, abuse, or torture other students should be held accountable for their actions and disciplined accordingly. However, in order to truly stop hazing, we need not only to discipline and punish but also to understand why perpetrators do what they do.

How Does Someone Turn into a Perpetrator?

Most perpetrators learn how to haze by being victims themselves. Once they've been victimized, they swear to never be victimized again, especially if the hazing was extreme. This is where the virus of anger and revenge begins and simmers for years. The fury of having been violated increases as the student becomes a bystander. Consciously or unconsciously, he waits for the moment when he will have power, control, status—the moment he will become a perpetrator. Finally, when the student is in a position of authority and has the ability to discharge his violent feelings of revenge, he acts out his aggressions.

Acting aggressively on someone else completes the metamorphosis from victim to bystander to perpetrator and allows the student to move on. This metamorphosis allows the student to psychologically retrieve the part of himself that was lost when he was degraded or humiliated during his original hazing. Once this experience has been completed, perpetrators often feel whole, in control. I call this pattern the *blueprint of hazing*. Frequently, the student packs up these experiences and puts them into his backpack as he heads off to college, the military, or the workplace, with the expectation that he will be hazed and will haze again.

In this subtle way, a student's personality has been changed, becoming ever more hostile and sadistic, as he has experienced the violence, enjoyed his ability to influence others, and exercised his power over the group. The power gives the perpetrator a heady feeling, the sense that he is invulnerable, untouchable, and safe, no matter the situation. This attitude is consistent with the typical adolescent belief that nothing bad can happen to them.

This depth of denial is an earmark of adolescence and young adulthood. Their need to discharge their aggressive impulses, coupled with the belief that they are somehow protected from danger or the law, allows them to lose control, to haze without realizing the consequences or acknowledging their responsibility. Even after they've been arrested, perpetrators usually don't accept responsibility for their actions. They identify as part of a group and are not fully conscious that they'll be held responsible as individuals.

Sometimes perpetrators are truly aggressive, impulsive people who lose their temper easily and actually get pleasure in hurting or ridiculing others. These students may have been abused themselves or have real pathological conditions. Sometimes these very aggressive individuals are the best athletes and achieve positions as captains and group leaders. These students are also given tremendous respect, power, and control by their peers, coach, team, and community. On the field, their aggression is sublimated into a winning play, but in the locker room the aggression is misdirected and unchecked. This further encourages the hierarchical nature of the group and gives these impulsive individuals license to behave in aggressive and sexual ways without fear of consequences.

This is the very circumstance that occurred in the story about the Mepham hazing from Chapter One. The key perpetrator had a long history of suspensions and had even threatened a freshman before the group went to the football camp. It's under these kinds of circumstances that the adult crew, the coaches and leaders, must increase their supervision. Students who are known to have a history of acting-out behavior or other emotional problems must be kept under constant adult supervision and surveillance. Simply hailing the star athlete as the best, without protecting him and the team from his own impulsive behaviors, is detrimental to the well-being of everyone involved.

Although some perpetrators enjoy being aggressive, degrading others, and flaunting their superior status or strength, many other perpetrators are conflicted in their role as leader.

These perpetrators may have passed on the tradition of hazing due to peer pressure. They do what is expected of them as senior members of the group—even if it's contrary to their own personal values. They may have been ambivalent or even against the activities. Perhaps they expressed their views, and they were outvoted, or they never told anyone about their thoughts.

Perpetrators often are not held responsible for their actions, and the traditions continue without question. So each time a hazing is not reported, a new group of students is conditioned to believe that they too will not be held responsible for their actions as perpetrators. This gives students a false sense of security, reinforces the tradition, and plants the seeds for a new hazing and new perpetrators. Each time perpetrators are not appropriately disciplined, each time they get a mere slap on the wrist, we, as parents, teachers, and coaches, are accepting the hazing activities and condoning the behaviors.

> ➤ **DID YOU KNOW** ⤙

According to the Alfred University study, many high school and college students don't distinguish between "fun" and hazing. Forty-eight percent of students participated in activities that meet the definition of hazing, although only 14 percent said they were actually hazed. Most students that participated in potentially illegal or hazardous hazing activities did so because they were fun and exciting.[4] In my study, 89 percent of fraternity and sorority members don't believe that disturbing things happen during an initiation ritual. This gives insight into how students perceive danger.[5]

How Can Someone Be So Cruel?

Hazing provides a seemingly, socially acceptable excuse for expressing violent, sexual, or sadistic behaviors. Because of this, most perpetrators don't perceive their actions as cruel. In their minds, they are simply repeating the tradition of the group, in many cases, the same tradition they went through when they first joined. Even when their victims are hospitalized or sexually assaulted, they still don't see the hazing as sadistic. They see it as a tradition that proves one's worthiness. This is why they can be so cruel: they change the parameters of what is considered *acceptable* during a hazing. They don't use the same criteria to evaluate their own behavior, within a hazing event, as they would if considering the same actions in a different, non-hazing situation.

The same thing happens for both male and female perpetrators. They temporarily suspend their moral code and act as though their behavior *does not count*. Traditions that include exposing genitals, imitating sexual acts, using fingers and objects to sodomize, branding with cigarettes and irons, and being collared and led on a leash are completely acceptable within the context of a hazing tradition.

I doubt that anyone would willingly participate in these highly aggressive and sexual activities if it weren't part of the hazing process. In fact, in any other circumstance, the student would consider these kinds of actions to be abusive and would probably call 9-1-1 to report them.

Perpetrators often add a new twist in order to personalize the experience, making the event slightly different. Adding one's own personal touch is part of the competition to "out-do" the group before them. As each group adds their own special style, such as increasing the amount of alcohol consumed or calisthenics performed, they are adding the elements that lead the hazing into a more dangerous zone. With each increase of activity, the likelihood of trouble is also increased, especially because the leaders don't stop to think about the effects of the change. They don't evaluate the activities for danger; instead, they evaluate them for excitement, degradation, or humor.

In addition, perpetrators may suffer from a *failure of empathy*. Psychologists use the term to explain how some people are not able to imagine how another person is feeling. Perpetrators envelop themselves in the protective coating of the group, one that allows them to believe they're all powerful. Under these conditions, the perpetrator and group suspend reality and create a situation in which it's acceptable to haze. The perpetrator doesn't put himself in the shoes of his victim and doesn't consider what the experience might be like for the other person. If he sees a victim crying or upset, he might increase the hazing, causing more pain and suffering. The perpetrators perceive the tears as an indication of weakness. They want teammates to be tough, like they are. "Not being able to take it" stimulates feelings of inadequacy in both the victim and the perpetrator.

It's possible that at a different time, under totally different conditions, the same perpetrator might be understanding, reaching out to someone who appears to be stressed or upset. It's difficult to understand how the same person could have such different reactions. The answer lies in the fact that judgment, values, and morality are suspended during a hazing.

An Insider's View of Hazing

Hazing is an important part of sorority initiations. It helps girls bond, become closer, and brings the pledges to a mindset of belonging to the group. My sorority hazed, but not to the degree of anything dangerous. Save for disciplinary paddlings on the rare occasion that a sister breaks a core value, this is the limit to our physical hazing. There are many projects that a pledge must complete to become a sister, and all have important value. Being paddled is only one of the dozens of steps taken in the journey. In the end, they prepare for the paddling by accepting that it is a welcoming into the structure of the sorority and the sisterhood. After a week, the bruises are gone. No serious injury has ever set in. A paddling is a submission to the greater group. Stripping naked, bending over, and allowing someone to inflict pain is an acceptance of your giving in your will as an individual to authority of the group you wish to be part of. It's embarrassing, it hurts, and most girls, including me, cry their eyes out when it happens to them. It is not however abuse, it's not mean, and it shouldn't be criminal. I feel that if you want to be part of the group, you have to take your medicine just like every other woman who has been through it.

—ANONYMOUS E-MAIL sent to my Web site

HOW YOU CAN HELP A PERPETRATOR

Perpetrators, like bystanders and victims, are in need of psychological help and parental support. No matter how disappointed you feel or how humiliated you are by your child's actions, it's now that he needs you the most. This is a critical time for you to bond. It's also a critical time to teach some lessons, instill new moral codes, and help your child mature into an adult who will not continue to be a perpetrator. It's your attitude and your ability to focus on the "big picture" that will help him through these rocky times, which may determine his future.

Dealing with Your Child's Emotions

If your child has been accused of being a perpetrator in a hazardous hazing, it's likely that he'll face various kinds of criminal charges, the least of which is hazing.

This may cause your child to be in a state of shock and emotional confusion. He may not have intended to cause such problems. His memory of the events, the way he understood the situation, may be unclear and not seem to match the accusations. In addition, he may have been in an altered state, due to alcohol or drugs, during the time that he was involved in the hazing.

When a perpetrator has been charged and is being held responsible for hazing, it's probable that he'll be full of anger, feeling unjustly punished. He may claim that it was not his fault; he was merely repeating the tradition. He might blame others in the group, who may have participated but weren't charged. He may also feel betrayed by the group, by the victims, by the person who broke the code of silence, and by the coach or leader for not protecting him from the charges.

Parents need to stabilize the situation by allowing their child to vent. The child should be encouraged to talk about his point of view. Writing in a journal or speaking with close family and friends will help him express his thoughts in a constructive manner and help diminish some of the anger. Keeping the child's aggression in check is key, but this may be difficult for the perpetrator and his family. But using threats, intimidation, or acting out against the victims or bystanders will ultimately cause further harm to your child. It's at this point that a neutral outsider, such as a psychologist, is helpful. Individual as well as family counseling may be recommended. Remember, this is a crisis and intervention is necessary.

Sometimes a perpetrator feels remorseful, realizing the pain and suffering that he has caused. Perhaps he's embarrassed by his own actions. A reactive depression may occur when he realizes the ramifications of his actions. The depression may be noticed in his mood, irritability, feelings of betrayal and mistrust, or in his negative view of everything. This depression might be a normal response to the events that are occurring. Nonetheless professional intervention, such as psychotherapy, is recommended.

The depression may be entwined with anxiety and fear about the future. Anxiety is a normal reaction, although it may become too intense to tolerate and may interfere with the child's ability to function. As with depression, anxiety should also be treated. If professional counseling is not available, help might be obtained through the school, local hospital, court system, clergy, or privately through your health insurance. A perpetrator is often suffering, so it's important that these interventions are sought out.

Dealing with Your Anger

Crisis intervention within the family begins the moment you learn about your child's involvement. The entire family often experiences humiliation once the incident becomes public. Outrage is also a common emotion. Some parents are angered at their child for being engaged in the hazing activities. Other parents are angered that their child is being held responsible for a tradition that's been accepted by the community for years. Denial of your child's participation of the events is a common reaction. In fact, the entire town may support your view of the circumstances, because, in fact, the students may have been repeating a tradition that occurred for decades.

Anger is a strong emotion and everyone—the perpetrator, his family, and the community—feels it. Please remember:

1. *Be the parent.* Handling anger is not easy for anyone, especially under these circumstances. But someone needs to be in con-

trol and that someone is the parent! Psychologically, everyone needs help to stabilize, reduce the level of emotion, and then evaluate the situation in a calm, realistic manner. You must be the role model, the leader who will light the way. Assuring the family members that "together we will weather the storm" will keep everyone grounded and start the healing process.

2. *Don't lose control.* As a parent, you may feel that your child deserves a strong punishment for getting himself in so much trouble. Maybe you want to hurt him, and certainly you feel humiliated by his behavior. Maybe you feel betrayed by him, because you trusted that he had enough good sense to know right from wrong. Simultaneously, the perpetrator—your child—may also be full of rage and anger toward those who reported the hazing. This combination of heightened emotions is likely to lead to more trouble.

You need to consider how to let out your anger in a safe way. Create your own support system, so that you can model being in control of your own anger, because this is the very behavior that you need to teach your child. Find people to whom you can vent— professionals, such as psychologists or clergy, family or friends.

3. *Walk in the victim's shoes.* Many parents become angry at the victims and their families for breaking the code of silence and reporting the events. From this point of view, the parents completely support the hazing activities and are immensely angry at those who are accusing their child of doing something illegal or unjust. If you, as the parent, continue this attitude, you are reinforcing your child's violent actions. If you can't acknowledge that these actions were inappropriate and illegal, then how can you expect him to recognize his own mistakes? Supporting your child doesn't mean that you too have to suspend your own morality.

If you are having trouble accepting this, consider the following: What if a group of seniors surrounds your freshman child in a high school bathroom. As part of a high school initiation, they hold him down, slap his belly until it's bloody and bruised, and then sodomize him. Would you report the incident? Would you want to see the seniors disciplined for their actions? Would you hold the administration responsible for allowing your child to be humiliated and sexually assaulted and for placing him in a life-threatening situation?

Understanding Your Child's Leadership Status

As an outstanding athlete, fraternity president, or other kind of leader, your child has tremendous power to influence how others think and act. This power is part of the reason that he became a perpetrator and may be part of the reason that the hazing skidded into the hazardous zone. Now is the time to help him recognize his power and help him decide whether he wants to continue to be an intimidating force, hoping that the court of public opinion will vindicate him, or to use his power to stop hazing.

You need to help your child understand that hazing is too dangerous to continue and that he can be a positive role model for others. This concept is similar to what some former drug addicts have done. They turn their lives around, become clean and sober, and lecture students in middle and high schools about the dangers of drug and alcohol abuse. This concept is certainly applicable to hazing. In fact, the judge who presided over the Walter Jennings hazing case in 2003 required, as part of the sentencing, that the perpetrators make a documentary, focusing on the hazing that killed Walter. This film, *Unless a Death Occurs*, is used as an anti-hazing tool on college campuses throughout the country. The judge in Matt Carrington's hazing case has done the same thing, requiring the perpetrators to participate in anti-hazing programs.

Please understand that you and your child have the power to help the healing begin. You could speak with the victims, expressing your sorrow for the events and for the pain and suffering that they've endured. Though you may not directly say, "My child did it," you can say, "I am really sorry for what happened. No one intended any real harm to come to you." Rather than leading a negative campaign toward the victims, you can embrace them, sending the signal to the community that the hazing was indeed wrong, the tradition should change, and a compromise or peaceful settlement can be made. Setting up some kind of hazing prevention or intervention program could be part of the agreement made with the victims, thereby satisfying their needs, while avoiding possible criminal and legal complications.

Victims don't necessarily want revenge or compensation. They simply want to be acknowledged, their experience validated, and then some expression of sorrow, so that all can be forgiven and life can return to normal for everyone. Most parents don't want to ruin the lives of other children, even perpetrators. But they do want justice. They want to feel safe and hear that the traditions will not continue and others won't be hurt.

Preparing for Legal Issues

Regardless of a perpetrator's state of mind, his prior hazing experiences, the mind-set of the group that hazed, or the sentiment of the community, a perpetrator is responsible for his actions and may be held liable for the physical and psychological damages incurred by the victims. Even if the victims agreed to participate in the hazing, they did so without consent to be seriously harmed. Although the group as a whole may also be culpable, it's important to investigate and to acknowledge the possible legal consequences for your own child.

One of the first questions to ask is whether an attorney should be involved.

From my point of view, an attorney should be hired as soon as possible. You probably will need a criminal defense attorney, and you should try to find one who has experience in similar kinds of cases. Even if a lawsuit doesn't occur, an attorney is knowledgeable and may offer helpful support with other legal issues and dealings with the media.

A perpetrator may face several different kinds of legal issues depending on the severity of the hazing and the governing body in which the hazing occurred, such as a school, athletic league, or social organization. Each organization will have its own method of dealing with the events, from suspending a student for a short time, to ending the entire season for a perpetrator and team, to kicking a fraternity off-campus. Other consequences, such as the coach losing his job or other people being sued, may occur as well.

There are two kinds of possible lawsuits. A criminal suit is investigated by the police that govern the location of the incident. In addition, the victims and their families may sue in civil court. A civil suit is used to gain monetary relief for the pain and suffering caused by the perpetrators. These and other legal issues can start immediately after the hazing; however, they usually don't end for years. Often the tension and anxiety associated with these trials are difficult for everyone: the victims, the bystanders, and the perpetrators.

Of course, this is only the tip of the iceberg. There are many other legal issues and details to consider and investigate. See the Resource Guide at the back of the book for further information.

Being the parent of a perpetrator is probably a role that you never considered before it actually happened. It tests you in terms of your own self-control and your ability to understand your child, the situation, the rituals, the law, and the response from the community. As a parent, you might find it difficult to accept your child's behavior, and it might be difficult to forgive and support him. This will take tremendous strength, energy, time, and financial resources. Regardless of the part that your child had in the hazing, it's important that you stand by him, helping him to understand his role in the incident and providing him with the appropriate protection.

6

Empowering Bystanders

It began as a typical party in Dallas, Texas, on August 27, 2005. Twenty freshmen were welcomed onto the wrestling team of the Flower Mound High School. Parents of the fourteen-year-olds dropped their kids off at the home of one of the teammates, not knowing what was in store for their sons. The fifty upperclassmen stripped the newcomers down to their bathing suits and gave them pink bellies, *by slapping them repeatedly. Then they threw the younger boys into the pool. The older, larger boys wouldn't let the freshmen escape, dunking them back into the pool, as other players, the coach, and some parents allegedly watched. There were stations where various hazing events occurred, including throwing footballs at the heads of the freshmen;* knifing, *in which someone was surprised by being whipped in the rear; and* chicken fighting, *in which freshmen were placed on the shoulders of seniors and long, foam noodles (pool floats) were used as swords, which left significant welts and black-and-blue marks. In addition, team members sexually assaulted at least one freshman, using condom-covered fingers to penetrate him. Five victims were sent to the hospital, one had a concussion, and another had a bruised spleen. The coach was fired and charged with hazing, and eighteen students were charged with assault and hazing, three of whom were charged with felony sexual assault. The community was extremely agitated by the hazing charges and by the loss of a beloved coach, who was 2004 Wrestling Coach of the Year in all of Texas. Many parents felt that this party should be categorized under "boys will be boys" rather than a hazing.*[1]

It's easy to identify the victims and perpetrators of a hazing, but who are the bystanders? What is their role in a hazing? Are they affected by what they witness, and if so, how? Like the middle child, bystanders are often overlooked. However, they're extremely important in terms of the group dynamics and are a necessary ingredient in most hazing incidents. It's also at this stage in the cycle of hazing that the most important intervention can take place. It's incumbent on each parent and coach to help a child at this juncture. This chapter aims to give you insights into the power of the bystander and how you can help students feel their strength and turn it into action.

UNDERSTANDING THE BYSTANDER

Bystanders witness events as they occur but don't actively participate. All of us have been bystanders at some point, whether it's witnessing a traffic accident or watching breaking news on TV. Most of us were bystanders as we watched the Twin Towers collapse and Hurricane Katrina devastate New Orleans. In these two instances, much of the country and the world responded with a huge outpouring of emotions and aid. Why? As we watched these events unfold, we had a strong emotional need to help. By doing so, we were identifying with the victims, thinking something to the effect, "There but for the grace of God, go I." We felt empathy and expressed it by giving and reaching out to the victims. We were active bystanders and had strong feelings that stayed with us for a long time, even though we didn't actually participate in the events.

In contrast, most bystanders of a hazing, including those at the Flower Mound party, which included both students and adults, don't seem to have the same feelings or empathy. The Flower Mound bystanders didn't recognize the party as something dangerous and didn't interpret the "horseplay" as hazing. Not even the Flower Mound wrestling coach, who wrote the anti-hazing rules for the team, seemed to realize that the older boys were hazing the newcomers. Perhaps that's why they didn't intervene, didn't stop the action, didn't protect the victims.

How Does Someone Become a Bystander?

In hazing, the victim usually becomes the bystander and the bystander becomes the perpetrator. In this metamorphosis of a group, one moves from newcomer to the next stage of seniority, of having some status but not the full status and power of a leader. The bystander is halfway through his informal training on how to haze. He has either been victimized or been a potential victim and has contracted some of the violence perpetrated by the group. He may be fortifying himself, identifying with the perpetrators, and waiting for his chance to haze others. Or he may be disgusted with the process and be considering ways to avoid becoming a perpetrator.

The bystander usually doesn't understand his role, his choices, or himself. He may not realize or believe he has the power to make a different choice and change the events he is witnessing. This isn't so different from the many moral and ethical dilemmas all of us face from time to time. If you have ever watched a parent spank, threaten, or abuse a child or family member or witnessed someone being discriminated against based on race, religion, gender, or ethnicity, you were the bystander, feeling helpless or concerned, or perhaps you felt it was none of your business. You may want to intervene, to stop the events from happening, but you're unsure of what to do. Most frequently, bystanders do nothing and let the events take place in front of their eyes, even if they are horrified by what they see.

Bystanders Are Stuck in the Middle

Bystanders seem to have the easiest role in a hazing. They are not getting hurt or creating the pain. The role of the bystander may seem simple, but it's not. The bystander is stuck. Should he report the hazing, even prevent it from happening? Should he keep everything secret and continue the ritual? If he does break the code of silence, will he be in danger? If he doesn't stop the events, will he be in danger? The bystander believes that he is stuck in a no-win situation.

Active bystanders tend to cheer on the perpetrators, often increasing the intensity of the moment. These students are enjoying the hazing, identifying with the aggressors, the perpetrators, as an audience does during a boxing match. Such students may have no dilemma; they don't want to stop the hazing or report the events. Active bystanders deny the fact that the ritual is a hazing and will likely continue the tradition when they have power in the group. They believe that they have the right and duty to continue the tradition and usually see it as a positive experience.

Passive bystanders are the most psychologically vulnerable because they are likely to be upset by the hazing. The passive bystander identifies with the victims and is stuck between wanting to run and hide and wanting to expose the hazing. Those who wish to hide are afraid that they might be hazed themselves. Bystanders that recognize the hazing activities as wrong and dangerous may not know whom to turn to. Often the passive bystander perceives himself as having little power or control, which increases his anxiety about reporting the hazing, even anonymously.

UNDERSTANDING THE BYSTANDER'S POWER

The key to hazing prevention lies in the bystander. The bystanders have significant power, both physically and psychologically. Physically, they are usually the majority and have the most strength when

---

An Insider's View of Hazing

My two daughters, ages ten and seventeen, and I went to pick up their brother from band camp. When we arrived, we saw a crowd with cameras and assumed they were taking pictures for the last day of camp. When we walked over, we noticed students had been saran-wrapped to the light pole outside the band room. One student was pouring a bottle of water over the wrapped students, and another, a can of Mountain Dew. My younger daughter looked at me and said, "Mom, this isn't right," and a parent standing nearby remarked, "There's nothing wrong with this, it is just good, clean fun." I turned to her and said, "No it isn't, it's hazing and it's against the law." I immediately looked for the band director but could not find him among the students or parents watching the event. To my amazement, all of this was being videotaped by a parent, while several other parents were watching and laughing with the students.

My two daughters were adversely affected by what they saw. My older daughter felt sick to her stomach and left to go back to our car. My younger daughter was afraid to go to school. They were both feeling the trauma of witnessing something very wrong happening.

—BEVERLY, mother of students who were bystanders during a hazing

---

acting as a group. A good example of this power is United Flight 93, which was scheduled to fly from Newark to San Francisco on September 11, 2001. On that crisp, clear morning, the flight was rerouted by terrorists who intended to crash the airplane into the Capitol Building in Washington, D.C. Once the passengers learned of their fate, they organized and changed their roles, from passively watching to actively fighting back. Their power didn't come from weapons or training, but from the individuals who gelled into a cohesive group with a specific purpose. They died heroes, heroes to teach us all that we have power as bystanders.

Psychologically, a group of bystanders have the power and control to push the situation in or out of balance. If they recognize their power, as the bystanders on United Flight 93 did, then they can use their insight to stabilize the situation and to lead the group into a more positive place. In fact, as bystanders become aware of their power and are able to coordinate their efforts as a subgroup, it's possible that they will choose to change the blueprint of hazing, by not becoming perpetrators. It's your job, as a parent, teacher, or coach, to have each student recognize his power and responsibility.

Bystanders are like designated drivers. A designated driver accepts the responsibility to stay sober, maintain good judgment, and get everyone home safely. Bystanders during a hazing can do something very similar. Because they don't actively participate, bystanders can maintain a cooler state of emotions and keep the best interests of the group in mind. They should be the sobering voice, reminding the group of the possible consequences of continuing any dangerous activities.

Why Should the Bystander Be Empowered?

The bystander often becomes the perpetrator in the next hazing. Before that happens, we can empower the bystander to take a stand and choose not to repeat the cycle of hazing. This is a good opportunity to teach children life lessons they can use immediately. By teaching empathy for the victims, instilling a strong moral code, and reinforcing your values and beliefs, you can give the bystander the tools to choose to stop hazing before it even starts.

In addition, bystanders often share in the outcome of a hazing. For example, a bystander may also be punished when the entire group is suspended, the season is canceled, or the fraternity is closed. Often bystanders are interviewed and sometimes held responsible for not reporting the hazing. It's important to teach bystanders that there are also concrete motivations for reporting and stopping hazing, before, during, and after it occurs.

How Can the Bystander Become Empowered?

It's important to teach kids appropriate methods and skills they can use to tap into their own moral values. For hazing, this means giving kids the tools to know how and when to report an incident. For bystanders, there are two ways, as an individual bystander or as a group of bystanders. It's VITAL for you to clearly differentiate this with your child. Please read the next section carefully!

An individual bystander should always remember not to confront the perpetrators directly. This would put him in a possibly dangerous situation. Your child's safety is paramount.

As an individual bystander, your child can report a hazing anonymously by any of the following ways:

1. Calling a tip hot line. Hazing hot lines exist in many colleges and universities across the country. (Cornell University has created an excellent model for this that can be viewed at www.hazing.cornell.edu.) In fact, in recent years, more time and resources have been given to empower students to report guns, drug, violence, or gang-related activities at their schools. Even if the college or school district doesn't have a hot line specific to hazing, a student should use the hot lines that are available to him (such as a crisis intervention hot line). Local and campus police also have tip hot lines and voice mail services that students can use.

2. Posting information on a Web site set up by the school or organization or by using www.mashinc.org, or www.report-it.com.

3. Leaving a note in a suggestion box or sending a letter to a teacher, coach, school principal, administrator, campus police, or even the local police department.

In addition, an individual bystander can report a hazing in any of the following ways:

1. Speak to someone he trusts, in confidence, about any hazing-related activities. This might be a parent, teacher, coach, clergy, or other authority figure the student trusts. By doing this in confidence, the student's identity is not revealed, and the weight of the knowledge is transferred from the child's shoulders onto the shoulders of the adult confidante.

2. Speak directly to an authority figure without hiding his identity. To do this, the student would need to be very courageous and strong, as Jake Savoy was, whose story was told in Chapter Two. In this case, the child is revealing his identity, taking the mature and brave steps to inform the appropriate authority. If your child chooses this route, it would be most helpful for you to be supportive of his actions.

A *group of bystanders also has the ability to change the hazing traditions, if they work together.* Although it's not easy, the group has the power to stop hazings before they start or to end them before they skid into the hazardous zone.

How can you empower your child to safely organize bystanders to stop hazing?

1. Organize the group of bystanders, before a hazing, to work together. Suggest that your child speak with his peers and say something like, "Hey, we have to limit what goes on so no one gets hurt and in trouble. We don't want to lose the season (or the chapter) just because so-and-so gets out of control. We have to work together as a team, to make sure things remain 'chill.'" Make the analogy that bystanders are like the designated drivers for the group. They have a job and duty to protect each other.

2. Explain to the group how important their presence is to the hazing. Without the bystanders as an audience, there's less chance that the hazing will occur or that it will move into the hazardous zone. The group can use this knowledge to their advantage.

3. Create a plan of how to work with the group of bystanders to intervene during a hazing by calming the emotional climate and warning the perpetrators of possible consequences. Simultaneously, the group can try to release the victims from the state of bondage. They can do this by reminding the perpetrators of the following:

- There are hazing laws and consequences.

- People have died because of similar activities.

- Their judgment may be impaired due to alcohol or drugs.

- The bystanders are saving the perpetrators from criminal charges by stopping them before things get out of control.

- It's not worth it to the group to jeopardize their season, their group's status, or their leader's (for example, the coach) job or their own safety just to continue the activity.

When Should a Bystander Report?

A bystander can report individually or as a group, at many different times, under various scenarios. Here are some examples:

1. Before a hazing occurs, bystanders are usually aware of when and where it'll occur. Remember, groups often use the same locations repeatedly.

2. During a hazing, a group of bystanders can either try to intervene, or they can exit as a group and get help.

3. After the hazing, the individual or group can report the events, either anonymously or by allowing their identity to be

known. In some instances, it's in the bystander's best interest to have his identity known, showing that he's cooperating with the appropriate authorities to reduce the harm of the hazing.

4. Bystanders can report hazing at any time, even if the hazing occurred in the past. Although hazings usually occur at particular times of the year, such as at the beginning of football season, reporting the hazings will help authorities educate and intervene in the future.

HOW YOU CAN HELP A BYSTANDER

As a parent of a bystander, you too may face a moral dilemma. You know that your child was present during the hazing. Should you allow him to come forward and tell the truth? Are you protecting him from harm by ordering him not to tell? What is in the best interest of your child?

If your child was a bystander during a hazing, it's important for you to remain calm and in control of your own emotions as you learn about the events. The details of the hazing may be shocking. You may also learn that your child has been a bystander more than once. For example, athletes in high school may be victims in their freshman year, but they are likely to be bystanders throughout their sophomore and junior years. Frequently, high school athletes participate in two or three sports, and each may have an initiation that involves hazing. That means that by the time such a student reaches the ripe old age of seventeen, he may have been a bystander six (or more) times!

In fact, you may be discovering a wealth of other information that you never considered or imagined. You may even learn that your child was also hazed in the past. Before you get extremely upset, realize that you're lucky to have learned about these events. Now you have the opportunity to help your child heal and intervene before your child becomes a perpetrator!

Dealing with Your Child's Emotions

As the bystander is repeatedly exposed to hazing, two things occur. The bystander seems to adapt to the situation, becoming less upset as he grows numb to the hazing and accepts the tradition of the group. However, unconsciously, seeds are being sown that could grow into some serious psychological problems. The psychological issues can include feelings of grandiosity, a sense of being invulnerable or above the law, impulsivity, anxiety, insecurity, inadequacy, guilt, shame, and despair. If your child was a bystander during a hazardous hazing that involved sexual assault or even death, it's likely that the sights and sounds will haunt him—and perhaps you—in the present and in the future.

It's important to speak openly about the hazing situation, encouraging your child to tell you everything that he saw, heard, or knew. To do this, use some of the tips from the earlier chapters, in which you established open communication, reinforcing the feeling of trust between you and your child. All children want to tell; they need to uncork the hostility and anger, but they might feel the need to withhold the information to protect the group. It's here that you're at a crossroads. As adolescents, they want to separate and be mature, adult-like individuals, and simultaneously, they want to crumble in your arms and be protected from the big, bad world that suddenly thrust them into a horrible dilemma.

In order to promote dialogue, tell your child that it's a mature thing to confide in you and that in dangerous situations, such as a hazing, you'll work with him to come up with the best solution. Promise that you'll keep everything confidential and then you must do just that.

The most important task is for you to demonstrate to your child that you will always be there to help, that you understand his dilemma, and that you intend to support him.

Sometimes the feelings are overwhelming and evident; other times you may not even realize how differently your child is feeling or acting. The emotions come and go and sometimes invade your child's thoughts at the most random moments.

Bystanders may exhibit any of the following emotions:

- *Numbness* is perhaps the most difficult emotion for a parent to deal with because it indicates the child's unwillingness or inability to acknowledge the significance of the hazing that he has experienced. He may feel numb because he has seen so many people "take it" and he no longer can empathize with the victims. This numbness reflects the hard shell that's exactly what the perpetrators wanted to create. They want the members of their group to be mentally tough. The numbness is an indication that the student is on his way to becoming less sensitive to his own pain and to the suffering of others. It's an indication that his empathy has been reduced.

- *Anxiety* is a common symptom under these conditions. The bystander will feel anxious until he makes a decision about what to do, to report or not. However, he may continue to feel anxiety if he second-guesses himself, or if he is not supported by those around him, especially his family. He may develop sleep difficulties, nightmares, recurrent thoughts, fears, and phobias. The emotional tenor in the town may be very tense. It's possible that everyone is feeling anxious, including you. The question to consider is how much does the anxiety interfere with functioning. If it breaks through and reduces your ability or your child's ability to operate normally (go to school, go to work, maintain typical level of grades, and the like), then therapy should be considered . . . for parent and for child.

- *Depression* or negative thoughts, including insecurity, lack of confidence, and a loss of pleasure in doing things that used to be fun are indications that your child is in psychological pain. Again, intervention is important, even if it's only an evaluation to rule out serious problems.

- *Grandiosity* and feeling "above the law" is possible. Denial is often at the root of these reactions. These students are not willing or ready to see reality or face the possible consequences of their hazing activities. Like many adolescents, they believe that their parents don't know how things work and are out of touch. Unfortunately, these students are the ones who find themselves in trouble repeatedly or who need significant consequences in order to "learn the lesson."

Consider how much these emotions are interfering in your child's daily life. Is his sleep disturbed? Does he have nightmares? Has he begun to eat significantly more or less? Is his academic achievement declining? Has he become noticeably less social or isolated? Does he lack energy? Is he not enjoying things he used to? Is he more anxious and fearful, more reticent to do new things? If so, these are indications that he is in at least moderate turmoil and would benefit from some professional counseling.

To Tell or Not to Tell

The bystander and his parents are usually caught in the dilemma of what to do about reporting hazing activities. The moral lesson that you teach your child at this time will stay with him for the rest of his life. Your decision will affect you, your child, and your family—forever. Whatever you choose to do, you should understand that there are psychological repercussions.

> ➢ **DID YOU KNOW** ≺
>
> According to the Alfred University study, 36 percent of students surveyed wouldn't report a hazing because they believe there's no one to tell, and 26 percent felt that adults wouldn't handle the situation correctly.

The parent of the bystander who directs his child not to report hazing events may be doing so for several different reasons. A parent may believe, as his child believes, that the group's traditions and rituals are not really hazing or are not really dangerous. They take the boys-will-be-boys attitude. Often these parents have hazed and been hazed themselves and may even see hazing as a normal part of growing up. They view the trials and tribulations of a hazing as building character and endurance, and as a result they wouldn't want their child to break the code of silence.

Some parents may believe that their child should not report the hazing, but for a different reason—retribution. These parents are fearful and feel insecure about the social or legal ramifications that could follow. Parents of bystanders may consider reporting anonymously; however, even this may seem too risky. Parents themselves are sometimes ambivalent, because they are strongly pulled to do the "right thing" due to their moral and ethical beliefs, and simultaneously, they are insecure and anxious about the consequences. This dilemma is similar to the one that their child experienced as he observed the hazing.

Psychologically speaking, it's always better to tell rather than to hold in secrets. The bystander who has seen and heard but has not spoken will carry the hazing experience throughout his life. There's tremendous internal pressure created when children are prohibited from talking about something, such as a hazing. Though the symptoms of this pressure may never be obvious and may not be immediately noticeable, they are there. He is haunted for the rest of his life, wondering, Should I have done something, could I have done something?

The pain and suffering of the silent bystander increases as more and more information is repressed. If the bystander is exposed to a mild hazing, such as when male athletes dress in female clothing, he may not have any reaction. However, as the hazing events increase in humiliation, degradation, physical and psychological harm, it's likely that the pressure within the bystander will increase as well.

In addition, if we don't take actions to tell about hazing, it's likely that the activities will continue and worsen. If we don't intervene now, the ritual will be alive and well in the future, putting your younger child, your niece, or someone you know at risk. Where the arrow will stop, who will be seriously injured, is impossible to predict. So choosing not to do anything is like voting to continue hazing. Now that you know about how it escalates and how it does affect your child, it's your job to protect him and others. The way to protect your child—now and in the future—is to tell the truth.

Legal Considerations

The legal issues for a bystander are very different from what they are for victims or perpetrators. Although most bystanders are not held responsible for the hazing activities and will not need legal representation, they could still be involved in police or court proceedings. For example, when a hazing occurs in high school, everyone on the team, or in the group, might be interviewed. Sometimes, as in the Flower Mound hazing, at the beginning of the chapter, the findings are given to the police, and the individual stories are used as corroboration and to discover the truth about the event. Often students are interviewed without the prior permission of the parents. Their statements are sometimes entered into the police reports to be used in future court proceedings.

Bystanders also include adults who watched or had some overt or covert knowledge of the hazing. For example, in 2005 the Ontario Hockey League (OHL) fired the general manager and coach of the Windsor Spitfires after a hazing occurred on the team bus. The Windsor Spitfires had their rookies enter the *hot box*, which is the bathroom at the back of buses. Humiliating activities occurred as the athletes were stripped naked. Meanwhile their coaches sat in the front of the bus and did nothing to stop the hazing.[2]

In each of these cases, adults were either witnesses to the actual hazing events, or they enabled and encouraged the events to occur. Many more coaches were suspended or fired due to hazing in 2005 than in any previous year.

I believe that the answer to preventing hazing lies in the bystander. It may be difficult to understand that the people who are neither being hurt nor hurting are the most significant factor in the hazing dynamic. I hope that you've seen how bystanders, as a group, have the power to dominate, to tip the scale in favor of good judgment. As the parent, teacher, or coach, you have the responsibility for enlightening students about the power of the bystander. Each adult needs to be a great role model, demonstrating repeatedly that bystanders have power—and responsibility. This is a life lesson that you may just be realizing for yourself, but it's one that we must all teach our children.

7

Healing the Community

The pledge process at a small religiously affiliated college in Texas was typical in many regards. The nine pledges of the 2005 class served food at fraternity parties and cleaned up the messes, which included urine-and-feces-soaked kitchens. The girls performed sexually explicit songs and dances for the frat boys. They weren't allowed to call home. In order to walk on campus, pledges had to be escorted by three members of the sorority. All nine pledges were failing classes and feeling exhausted, overwhelmed, stressed, and depressed.

Kelsey, one of the pledges, had a particularly rough time with many of these rituals, because they undermined her own morals. The pledges were also kidnapped, blindfolded, and taken to a remote location to be tested on trivial information and made to do extensive calisthenics. This occurred nightly for weeks. Kelsey, upset and unsure of what to do, broke the sorority's rules by surreptitiously calling her mother and begging for help.

Kelsey's mom called the college and spoke to the student affairs administrator. She did so, anonymously, and was careful not to provide her name, her daughter's name, or any other identifying information. Unbeknownst to Kelsey's mom, the college somehow traced the call to her daughter. Shortly after this, the sorority was put on probation. Word of the phone call by Kelsey's mom made its way back to the other sorority members, and the sisters blamed Kelsey for the probation. From that moment, she was verbally harassed and physically threatened. She was cursed at in the cafeteria and other public places. Fistfights broke out, as friends tried to defend her. A Web page was also created by the sorority, which blasted and threatened her.

Because many of the sorority sisters were graduating in the spring, Kelsey hoped that the following fall semester would be better. It wasn't. Her lifetime friend from church, a new student, was told that she couldn't join any sorority because she was friends with Kelsey. Kelsey was told to leave campus during homecoming because the sorority alumni were coming, and she was likely to be hurt. Kelsey couldn't tolerate the isolation and harassment. She became depressed and was unable to study. She eventually dropped out of the college and lost her $20,000-a-year academic scholarship.

Unfortunately, Kelsey's story is an all-too-familiar reaction to a hazardous hazing: those who break the code of silence are often ostracized, becoming pariahs in their own communities. Many times, friends become foes, neighbors become enemies, and communities split and fracture. In fact, the aftermath of hazing can be just as devastating and dangerous as the hazing itself. Those siding with the victims or any bystanders that come forward are likely to be punished themselves. Those siding with the perpetrators are often in the majority and feel that the perpetrators have been unjustly accused. But the aftermath of a hazing doesn't have to be destructive. Even when dealing with a tragedy such as a hazing, communities can heal themselves and stay intact, forging new alliances and creating a safer environment.

This chapter is about the *second hazing*, the effects of it and the interventions that can be implemented. I suggest ways that you can become an agent of change, a person who'll turn the tide so that your community can heal and can stop hazing from reoccurring. Although the movement to curb hazing has just begun, we can already see change on the horizon.

THE SECOND HAZING

The aftermath of a hazing is very difficult for the victims and for those that break the code of silence. Rather than getting support or words of encouragement from their peers and neighbors, many victims are treated harshly and shunned from the community. The term *second rape* is used to describe how some communities treat a rape victim after details of the crime become public. It refers to the false assumption that the victim contributed to the rape by, for example, being in the wrong place at the wrong time or dressing in a provocative manner. Those investigating the rape, such as the police or school officials, doctors, nurses, and other professionals, may treat the victim with disdain and disapproval. The victim experiences this as a second rape. Rather than being supported, the victim is treated indignantly, which is why many rape victims don't report the event.

The victims of a hazing often feel the same way. Students who have been hazed feel violated by the perpetrators and then betrayed by their friends and community, who are often critical and unsympathetic. During the second hazing, the victims and their families are ostracized and isolated by those in the community. Often they are teased and accused of snitching. The victims, their families, and their supporters are made to feel as if they did something wrong, as though they invited the hazing or in some way caused the events to occur. The second hazing can continue for months and years, dividing communities and severing friendships. Those mistreating the victims underestimate the severity of the hazing, deny the psychological pain, and identify with the perpetrators, believing that the code of silence should not have been broken or that the victim is weak for simply not "taking it."

The second hazing begins as soon as the code of silence has been broken. Usually, there is an immediate, emotional response, in which many people vocally support either the victim or the perpetrators. In my experience, the perpetrators and their group leader, such as the sorority leaders or a team's coach, get the most support from the community. This spontaneous support begins the tide of ill feeling toward the victim. And sometimes it's even organized. For example, in Jake Savoy's case, discussed in Chapter Two, bright yellow T-shirts were printed, which read "Back Swack," in support of the coach and were worn by many parents to an away football game. Likewise, T-shirts supporting the wrestling coach in Flower Mound were also worn by many in the community.

Why Does the Second Hazing Occur?

The second hazing is a typical reaction after the code of silence has been broken. The leaders of the group try to distance themselves and the group from the specifics of the hazing event. The idea is to maintain the positive identity of the group. A report of a hazing is seen as an attack, and the natural response is to defend and counterattack. This response is what causes the second hazing. The fact that a hazing has occurred and has been reported threatens the group. In order to protect its image, many people in the group defend it by diminishing the significance of the hazing or by denying it completely. The more threatened the group feels, the stronger the defense.

The second hazing is also an unconscious response. Each individual identifies with someone in the hazing. For example, people who have been hazed or victimized have anger about their own experiences. It's likely that they'd feel sympathetic and understanding toward the victim and would want to be supportive, even if they weren't able to report their own abuse. In contrast, those who have hazed others or have been hazed themselves but accept the hazing as a way to prove worthiness and solidarity with the group will identify with the perpetrators. They'll feel sympathy and understanding for the hazers and the group's leader and will show support for them.

A dilemma exists for those in the community that may understand and support both points of view. For example, one of the victims in a hazing had two older brothers who had also played lacrosse at the same school and for the same coach. I talked with the oldest brother, who was in college, hoping to become a coach. It was clear that he felt that he had learned a tremendous amount from the lacrosse coach and had gained important experiences as a member of his team. However, he was emotionally torn because his youngest brother had been brutally hazed and violated. He knew this was wrong and that it was in some part the responsibility of the same coach, whom he had respected and revered. This young man had experienced the best and the worst that sports—and this coach—had to offer. Had it not been his brother who was harmed, he probably would have supported the coach and the perpetrators. But because it was his own brother, he supported the victim.

This story illustrates the fact that throughout hazing, individuals are torn and are placed in moral dilemmas. It's not necessarily easy to choose and support a particular side. The reasons that you do are a reflection of many components of your personality, your experiences, and your emotional state. It takes strength and courage to stand up to the majority, to support the underdog, and to go against the tide of public opinion.

Even if you have no direct tie to the hazing event or to the groups involved, you often feel supportive of one side. This is because you identify with the community as a whole. For example, in the St. Amant, Louisiana, case described in Chapter Two, everyone, regardless of age, felt that their town and their customs were under siege. The desire to rid themselves of negative media was quite strong. The townsfolk were angry at Jake and his family for bringing attention to the issue and threatening the status quo. These sentiments fueled the second hazing.

It seems impossible not to have an opinion once a hazing hits the news. If you check the responses on campus bulletin boards, or in local newspapers, there is usually a significant amount of chatter and many emotional comments. Almost everyone gets involved and chooses a side to support.

What Are the Effects of the Second Hazing?

The community, as a whole, is profoundly affected by the second hazing. In each case that I studied, the community was split. The hostility between those who supported the perpetrators and those who supported the victims was extreme, and it affected everyone negatively. Every corner of the small town experienced an aftershock. The second hazing is the community's response to the code of silence being broken. Because most groups don't want to be exposed and want to support the status quo, the energy unleashed during the second hazing is powerful. Friendships; family relationships; trust of the school, coach, and other groups are all threatened and often broken. The community needs interventions, and none are given. The scar within the community is deep, and the length of time that it takes to heal is immeasurable.

The victim, his family, and his supporters are all severely affected. They are often socially isolated and are dealing with the physical and emotional effects of the actual hazing, the subsequent strain of the media and legal system, and the gossip and disparaging looks from the community. Perhaps the part that hurts the most is the sense of betrayal. At this vulnerable moment, each member of the family needs the support of friends and family, and often these very people betray them—choosing to support the perpetrators. This betrayal is the last straw. The victim and his family have already felt betrayed by the students in the group (often friends or teammates), betrayed by the administration (who was supposed to protect the student), and now they feel betrayed by their friends and family.

The perpetrator and his family often have community support, which makes it easier for them to function. They see the tremendous

An Insider's View of Hazing

*My son was a victim of hazing. His message to other students
is "Don't let it get to you because it wasn't your fault."*

*I asked if he regretted telling us what happened, and he
said he had to tell us. His belief is that if he didn't tell, it would
have happened again to him or others and that wasn't right.
I truly believe he told because he knew that it was wrong and
that it had to stop. I cannot tell in words how proud I am of
my son's maturity. In some ways, he has handled this better
than my husband and I.*

*I personally wish people who are not directly affected by
an incident but feel strongly against hazing would stand up
publicly and support the victims. We really could use an un-
biased voice.*

—LISA, mother of a victim of a high school hazing

swell of local support as evidence that they were unfairly blamed and
that justice will be served. Sometimes their position will be legit-
imized after a legal investigation; however, in most cases, this is a
false hope. The perpetrators and their supporters often feel elated
and less anxious as a result of the second hazing. It's difficult for them
to understand the issues when much of the public agrees with them.
This makes it less likely that they'll see how they are responsible.

The bystander and his family could have another wave of worry,
deciding whom to support—the victim or the perpetrator. In some
cases, the bystander has been intimidated, directly or indirectly, by
the perpetrators. He may have been told not to speak, not to tell
the truth. In such cases, the bystander may feel that he is being
watched by those who threatened him and may support the perpetrators out of fear.

On the other hand, the bystander may feel strongly about the situation and might have clarity and insight. Though rare, such students will be able to choose the position that feels correct and comfortable to them.

The parents of the bystander will also be anxious, trying to decide how to handle the situation. Ultimately, the bystander and his family may support the larger group, usually the perpetrators, in order to diminish the backlash, retribution, or other negative effects that they fear will occur if they support the victims. The bystander and his family may experience anxiety, depression, or relief, during the second hazing.

Authority figures, such as coaches, school administrators, and sorority presidents, may have a sense of euphoria, as they are supported by the community. This positive energy reduces their own anxiety, depression, anger, and other negative effects that result when hazings are reported. As with perpetrators, coaches and administrators can view the support of the community as a sign that they're not really responsible or wrong.

Intervention Strategies

Eliminating the second hazing involves changing the way the community responds to the original hazing and how it deals with the crisis. Truthfully, change is slow and difficult, and it occurs when it's either wanted by the majority of the community or imposed upon them. The intervention strategies that I'm suggesting (see the following list) are intended to change the culture of the community, to heighten their awareness about themselves and how they support hazing, and to reduce the split within the community. Ironically, the community needs to do exactly what the team or fraternity originally intended with their hazing tradition. The community needs to bond and become committed to the true meaning of brotherhood!

It's incumbent upon you and your community to take the first steps. Consider implementing some of the following strategies to help make changes in your neighborhoods and schools. In addition, support local and national efforts to push hazing onto the radar screen of our elected officials, high school and college administrators, Greek alumni, professional sports teams, and manufacturers of sporting goods. When funding for research and prevention-and-intervention programs are supported by large institutions such as these, the chances of a cultural shift are increased.

Clearly, no change can happen until those teaching the leaders are themselves appropriately trained and able to employ effective methods. Professionals who receive hazing reports, including the medical staffs at hospitals and in private offices, as well as the police on campuses and in communities, need to be trained by hazing educators and psychologists on how to handle the reports and all of the individuals involved. The attitudes and opinions of the staffs often interfere with their ability to give the appropriate response and support to the individual who's reporting.

A protocol on how to process a hazing report should be created by each group that is vulnerable to hazing and to the group of professionals who are the first responders to a hazing. At a minimum, the protocol should take the following into account:

1. Those individuals who are receiving the report should understand that confidentiality is key. They must gauge the physical and emotional state of the *reporter,* in order to ascertain what level of intervention is warranted. They should be understanding and supportive. They should not share their own personal feelings, views, or experiences with the reporter. In other words, anyone who is dealing with the hazing should act in a professional manner.

2. An information chain of command should be established in advance with the method of communicating determined prior to a crisis; for example, cell phone or e-mail. For instance, www.report-it.com establishes a sequence of who within the school district or college should be notified first. In addition, how they are contacted and who else receives the report is also determined in advance. This

kind of planning increases the success of the program and reduces anxiety and miscommunication.

3. Mental health professionals need to interview all those involved, including perpetrators, bystanders, and their families, and provide support services, such as group and individual counseling.

4. The administration of the school or group should hold community forums to explain the details of the event and allow people to air their feelings and have their questions answered. Educators must explain what the second hazing is and teach the groups that this need not occur. In order to reduce the harmful effects of a hazing on all the students and their families, it's necessary for those in authority to send a loud and clear signal that they, as a school, group, or community, need to support one another rather than split into opposing factions. It's at these forums that programs can begin to heal the community, by having community leaders such as clergy, counselors, and other well-respected authorities offer appropriate services. Crisis intervention teams should be established prior to a hazing or other crisis. Local hospitals, mental health agencies, interfaith groups, social service organizations, and other community-based personnel should have appropriate support established so that informational sessions and support services can be immediately available and offered at these forums. Teachers, psychologists, and guidance counselors should help parents deal with their child's questions and issues.

The administrators of groups whose participants may be involved in initiations and hazing traditions, such as high school and college athletics and college fraternities and sororities, should do the following:

1. Develop a system that rewards those who report a hazing, reinforcing the idea that telling is the right thing to do. By recognizing the reporters as heroes, the community is sending a strong message that hazing is hazardous and won't be tolerated. By creating a

program that provides rewards, the community will demonstrate how important it is to break the code of silence. These actions will help reduce the basis of the second hazing.

2. Encourage members of the community with social status and power to support the healing process. Popular members of the community who have social standing due to their economic role, fame, or political power could lead meetings and rallies that support the concept that the community should stick together. Student leaders, those who have social status due to their athletic, creative, or academic strengths, should be asked by the administration to lead events as well.

3. Unite psychologists and other professionals from the community's mental health agencies, as well as from the government and private sector, to form a hazing treatment coalition. This kind of coalition should direct and provide various kinds of services to meet the needs of the community. The psychological support services are of critical importance to the success of these programs.

In addition, community organizations and institutions, such as police, school districts, and colleges, can work with the media to help the community heal. Too often, local newspapers and television newscasts exacerbate the second hazing through their editorials. The media should disseminate the facts and exclude certain details, such as names and photographs of minors when appropriate. The media should be informed about the plans to prevent a second hazing, because they provide the best format for publicizing positive programs. They can be a great tool to stop the second hazing and help the community heal.

IS THERE HOPE?

It's difficult to imagine that there might be any hope for those of us who want to end hazing. After all, hazing seems to be part of human nature. Hazing occurs throughout the world and has occurred throughout the ages. Hazing may start in adolescence and continue through adulthood. Is there hope? Should we even try to stop it?

I was trained originally as a social scientist and was fortunate to have worked on an independent study with Margaret Mead, the founder of Cultural Anthropology. I believe her words still ring true:

"Never doubt that a small group of committed citizens can change the world. Indeed it's the only thing that ever has." It's this thought that drives me to continue to combat hazing, and I hope it will inspire you to consider how you can help. Communities can heal from hazing, but it takes the effort of several strong people. Many of the stories that you have read have been horrific and almost impossible to believe. But there's something to be gained from every hazing that's reported. I hope these stories will give you strength for the future.

The Mepham High School hazing described in Chapter One has resulted in many positive changes in the school's leadership and in its coaching staff since the time of the hazing. Some of the perpetrators have recognized the problems and have taken personal responsibility for their acts. They have apologized to the victims and have gained insight into themselves. Perhaps most important, at least for me, is that it was this case that led to my involvement in hazing. It's this case that enlightened me about the lack of psychological knowledge about hazing, and it's this case that turned me into a hazing activist. I hope Mepham will never be forgotten and that it will be used as a case that encourages all high schools to examine their teams and clubs.

Jake Savoy has settled the criminal and civil suits related to his hazing. He is now in college and is pursuing his dream of becoming a pilot. His mother, Karen, continues to be a hazing activist, responding to each mother who needs support after a student has been hazed, via her Web site, www.mashinc.org. Karen is responsible for bringing national attention to high school hazing. She has appeared on *Oprah*, in *Sports Illustrated*, and in many other national venues. Karen and Jake deserve a lot of credit. They had the strength, courage, and drive to fight the system. Karen's commitment has helped many other families. It has also helped me. Her openness and honesty helped me understand the many facets of hazing.

Steve, the hazing story discussed in Chapter Three, never went public with his story. Following his mother's anonymous reports, the fraternity was sanctioned by the university. In addition, the college spent more time and effort investigating and limiting the pledge activities of all the Greek organizations on campus. Steve and his mother have become agents of change, spreading the message that hazing is dangerous to one's emotional well-being. Steve teaches other students, and his mother works to inform parents, teachers, and administrators in middle and high schools. Steve summarizes his insight this way: "If you allow yourself to get hazed and buy in to what the hazers are telling you and follow without question, that is the same as being a coward because you fear not being part of the group. Courage is knowing that the group is wrong and you should speak against it, even if you are one voice against forty or fifty."

Zach, whose story you read in Chapter Four, has openly revealed the details of his hazing. He and his mother are working hard to change the laws in Kentucky and to change the way that the local school system works. Zach's mother has become an ardent hazing activist and has made efforts to create a statewide coalition to combat hazing in high school. Both Zach and his mom are trying to decrease the legal and educational roadblocks that face hazing victims.

Matt Carrington's hazing case, discussed in Chapter Five, has been settled in terms of the criminal investigation. Everyone pleaded guilty to a variety of charges and the perpetrators have begun to serve their sentences. The most significant aspect is that the judge and district attorney in Matt's case have required each perpetrator to participate in anti-hazing activities. Matt's parents are making a documentary, and they have a not-for-profit fund in his memory that will support anti-hazing programs. In addition,

Matt's mom has a committee of dedicated people who are spreading the anti-hazing message in schools throughout California. (For more information please visit: www.wemissyoumatt.com.)

Chapter Six highlighted the Flower Mound hazing, and changes have occurred instantly due to the hazing. The parents of the victims have requested anti-hazing education to begin in sixth grade, and such programs are being created and instituted. The parents of the Flower Mound victims have also become hazing activists and will continue to fight for a high school that does not tolerate hazing.

Kelsey, discussed earlier in this chapter, is still reeling from her experience. However, the college did impose restrictions to her former sorority. Meanwhile the coalitions of several National Greek organizations have been sponsoring anti-hazing symposiums and have been trying to change the mind-set of those who lead. They recognize the negative psychological, social, and economic effects of hazing, and they are increasing their efforts to educate their current members and alumni.

It's clear that there are changes afoot in the field of hazing. For example, in 2003, when I began my research, Google had fewer than 50 sites that mentioned hazing. Less than three years later, Google reports approximately 3,850,000 sites! On a daily basis, newspapers and television news report hazing in high schools and colleges, in the military, and in the workplace. Each time a hazing is reported, another person is given some strength to come forward and report his hazing experience. Each report chips away at the base of the culture that supports hazing. Chip by chip, we can band together to create an environment that supports our children, rather than one that intimidates and degrades them.

GOALS FOR THE FUTURE

I am an eternal optimist, and I bring this positive outlook to the issue of hazing. I believe that we have not yet "begun to fight." There are many changes to be made within each system: legal, educational,

> ➤ DID YOU KNOW ≺

Most students and adults believe there is hope. In my survey of students, parents, and coaches, most of them considered a variety of interventions that could help stop hazing. Specifically

- Eighty-nine percent thought it would help to inform the entire group that they would all receive significant consequences if any hazardous hazing occurs.
- Eighty-eight percent agreed that it's important to empower the bystanders, as a group, to overcome the perpetrators when they perceive things getting out of control.
- Eighty-eight percent believed that it's important to have the leaders acknowledge the old traditions and define the limits, discouraging the tradition from escalating.
- Eighty-eight percent agreed that the leaders should be held responsible for the outcome.
- Seventy-nine percent thought that each season, or year, should begin with a contract of hazing consequences.
- Seventy percent thought there should be an anonymous suggestion box, where anyone could inform leaders of events that are planned or happening that might be dangerous, physically or psychologically.
- Fifty-five percent thought that a film or other material should be presented before the season or semester begins, which would educate the groups about hazing.

athletic, Greek, social, and psychological. This next section includes concrete ideas to pave the way toward a society that is free from hazing. Each one of us has the power to promote change. I hope that you will discover an area that you can become involved with, an area that appeals to you, so that you can become a leader in the fight to end hazing.

Legal

Our current state laws on hazing are weak. The definitions of hazing are not clear and don't necessarily cover hazing in middle and high schools or hazing off college campuses. Each state needs to "clean up its act," by coming up with a pragmatic definition of hazing that includes the many situations in which hazing occurs. Current state laws, outside of Florida, lack teeth. If there are not significant legal consequences, the laws are not deterrents. In order to create appropriate legal consequences, many people, not just specific perpetrators, need to be held accountable.

There are too many diverse definitions of hazing. The jurisdictions for each entity, in terms of local policies and state laws, make it necessary to create a uniform definition and a uniform system to litigate hazing cases. Karen Savoy and I have proposed national legislation, known as the National Hazing Prevention Act (NHPA), which I hope will be adopted by the federal government. A federal anti-hazing law should be instituted. The NHPA would provide funding for a toll-free anonymous number to report hazing, as well as establish university-based centers to create prevention and intervention programs and to train professionals to implement them. For further details of this proposed legislation, please visit my Web site (www.insidehazing.com).

Middle Schools, High Schools, and Colleges

Anti-hazing education needs to begin in middle school, with emphasis during the eighth grade. We should not begin hazing education at an earlier age because most students aren't able to comprehend all of the issues before the age of twelve. The program should be integrated into the curriculum wherever possible, although it should be clearly included in health education and physical education classes. Hazing should be integrated into other subject areas, such as social studies and English. Contests, awards, and other special programs, including guest speakers, films, and discussions, should be ongoing, with special recognition of National Hazing Prevention Week, which occurs at the end of September.

On the high school level, these programs should continue, with emphasis during the freshman and senior year. Freshmen are the new kids on the block, so to speak, and are most likely to be hazed. They are the ones who need to know how to deal with hazing, how to report it, and how to form their own groups so that they will protect one another. Sophomores, juniors, and seniors are all involved in hazing, so it's imperative that the hazing policy be reinforced throughout high school, in various classes. High school seniors, especially in their spring semester, are very concerned about hazing in college. Many have heard stories about hazing in fraternities and sororities or on athletic teams. Sometimes they choose colleges to avoid these experiences. It's very important to teach high school students and their parents about hazing in college and perhaps in the military and the workplace.

The school system should provide training to those adults leading the after-school student activities, such as coaches and bandleaders. It's their leadership, their personal experiences, their attitudes, and their point of view that can determine the effectiveness of an anti-hazing program. Hazing has been incorporated into the fabric of athletics, fraternities, sororities, and other programs. Simply outlawing it will not eradicate it. Significant educational training must be mandated so that those on the front line can be confronted with their own attitudes. Those who have been hazed and have hazed others often don't notice how they communicate—covertly—that hazing is OK. This kind of program will require repeated exposure and significant consequences for those who continue the traditions of hazing.

Parent education is another huge part of an anti-hazing program. Although I believe that students should not be alerted to hazing until eighth grade, I think that parents of elementary school children should be educated about hazing early on. It's at this stage that the parents can be positive role models by, for example, demonstrating how a group can question an authority figure that is out of control. It's this kind of parent education that can change behavior and attitudes. It is at this time that parents can be taught how to organize so they can model the power of a group of bystanders. They can also get tips on when and how to educate their children about hazing.

On the university level, a variety of programs for reporting and intervening should be instituted. Providing immunity to those who report hazing or to those who rescue victims by bringing them to hospitals or getting them appropriate care should be considered. Ongoing training of the entire campus staff, with special attention to those involved in athletics, band, and Greek life, should be mandated. The most significant change needs to be in the attitudes and expectations of those in positions of leadership. Significant consequences for the staff must be made clear, so that there is sufficient reason for them to change their behavior.

Athletic, Band, Religious, Greek, and Other Community Organizations

Local club sports and other community organizations that provide group activities for children aged twelve and older should participate in anti-hazing education. The leaders and their assistants should be required to learn about hazing and how to prevent it. In addition, as part of joining the group, the parents and children should be required to report any suspicions of hazing. The methods of reporting hazing activities should be clearly defined and protect the identity of those reporting. Awards, rewards, and other positive reinforcement should be given to those courageous enough to report.

Societal and Community Efforts

Local companies, newspapers, and television stations should also coordinate public service announcements that support the anti-hazing message. National television, cable, and radio networks should actively participate in spreading the message. This is an important way to educate the public.

National and local leaders in sports, entertainment, and business should be encouraged to become anti-hazing activists. When high-profile, respected figures support anti-hazing programs by breaking the code of silence, they are modeling the very behavior we want to teach: reporting an incident is the right thing to do.

Psychological Efforts

Since 9-11, the psychological community has recognized how important its role is in treating individuals who are affected by trauma. Hazing is traumatic, and psychologists need to be trained on how to deal with this specific kind of experience. Psychologists need to be educated on recognizing the effects of hazing on the victims, bystanders, perpetrators, and their families and friends. In addition, well-coordinated community outreach should be instituted.

The mental health community needs to establish ways to work together so that the local and national agencies can support schools and colleges, as well as the individuals who have symptoms resulting from their hazing experience.

WHAT CAN YOU DO?

After reading this book, you know more about hazing than most professionals! So remember the adage "knowledge is power." Use your knowledge, interest, and energy to do some of the following:

1. Become involved in local groups, such as youth sports, parent-teacher organizations, school boards, other advisory committees. Question their policy on hazing. Make sure that they don't feel satisfied to simply say, "Hazing is not permitted." Ask about the programs that have been created to embed the anti-hazing message in all the students, teachers, and coaches. Make it clear that exposing people to one anti-hazing lecture is not enough to change the culture, not enough to be considered a serious or effective hazing education program.

2. Become a local or national hazing activist. Join the various groups and organizations that have been created to fight hazing (see Resource Guide). Volunteer to help these groups, even if only online, so that your voice is heard. Create your own chapters of organizations, such as MASH, and support National Hazing Prevention Week in your community.

3. Educate other parents, teachers, coaches, and students. Share your experience and your knowledge. Every time I say the word *hazing,* regardless of where I am, someone has a story to share. Hazing sometimes brings smiles and other times groans, but it always creates an emotional response. You are the change agent; you are able to spread the message. Do it whenever possible.

4. Acknowledge the power of the bystander. Notice when you are a bystander, when your child is, and when others are. Demonstrate the power that the individual and the group of bystanders have.

Share the story of United Flight 93 on 9-11. Recognize these passengers as bystanders and heroes. (Watch and show the DVD called *The Flight That Fought Back.*) Support others by showing them the power they have as a group, as well as the responsibility they have to act positively to prevent hazing. Pressure schools and organizations to create programs that empower the bystander.

5. Write, write, and keep writing to the media when hazing is reported, to online message boards and other Web sites when hazing is discussed, and to your elected officials to press for better laws.

6. Talk, talk, and keep talking about hazing. The more aware others become, the more likely it is that the culture will change. The more empowered you are, the more empowered your friends and family will be. The more that hazing is exposed, the more it is reported, the less likely it is to continue to thrive.

Each time that an adult—parent, teacher, coach, or other leader—becomes enlightened about his or her role in hazing, an opportunity is created to teach, prevent, and intervene in the next hazing. Changing the attitudes of adults is as important as changing the attitudes of students. Each person, each bystander, each victim, each perpetrator, has tremendous power to influence others, to have them consider the negative effects of hazing on the individuals, the group, the community, and the future.

If our local and national leaders dedicate time, money, and effort to creating effective anti-hazing programs, our ability to increase awareness and educate the public will be improved. Each one of us is a potential agent of change. Each one of us has the capability to change our culture, to question authority, to create healthy environments, and to decrease hazing.

I invite you to join the small group of committed professionals, parents, and students who are fighting for a time and place in which hazing will be something we read about in history books, rather than in current news reports.

Notes

Introduction

1. For a detailed account of the Ambonwari adolescent ritual, please see "Being and 'Non-being' in Ambonwari (Papua, New Guinea) ritual." http://www.findarticles.com/p/articles/mi_qa3654/is_199706/ai_n8782933/pg_6.

2. http://depthome.brooklyn.cuny.edu/classics/dunkle/athnlife/homosex.htm#socrates.

3. Hank Nuwer, *Wrongs of Passage: Fraternities, Sororities, Hazing, and Binge Drinking* (Bloomington: Indiana University Press, 1999).

4. www.british-history.ac.uk/report.asp?compid=22134.

5. www.thecrimson.com/article.aspx?ref=507061.

Chapter One

1. Alfred University Study. http://www.alfred.edu/hs_hazing/.

2. Mothers Against School Hazing. www.mashinc.org.

3. Alfred University Study.

4. Karla Schuster and Keiko Morris, "How the Attacks, and Fear, Escalated," *Newsday* (p. A3–A57, Dec 18, 2003).

Chapter Three

1. www.massgeneral.org/news/releases/052402hazing.htm.

Chapter Four

1. Lipkins Hazing Study. Available at www.insidehazing.com.

2. Alfred University Study.

3. Cari Hammerstrom, "TEA Report on Former Donna Coach Telling," *The Monitor* (July 1, 2005).

4. Erica Rodriguez and Noah Bierman, "Hazing Closer to Being a Crime as Florida Advances Tough Law," *The Herald* (April 28, 2005).

Chapter Five

1. Mark Lore, "Fraternal Instincts," *Chico News & Reviews* (pp. 16–21, March 10, 2005); Terry Vau Dell, "Cuffed and Jailed: Fraternity Brothers Sentenced After Guilty Pleas in Hazing Death," *Chico Enterprise-Record* (October 28, 2005).

2. Karen Savoy, www.mashinc.org.

3. Nuwer, *Wrongs of Passage* (rev. ed., 2001); Nuwer, *A Weed in the Garden of Academe* (forthcoming, 2007).

4. Alfred University Study.

5. Lipkins Hazing Study.

Chapter Six

1. Brandon Formby and Jay Parsons, "Teacher, Students Turn Selves In," *Dallas Morning News* (September 15, 2005); Jay Parsons and Brandon Formby, "Was It Hazing, or Just Boys Being Boys?" *Dallas Morning News* (September 17, 2005).

2. "Windsor Saga Finally Draws to a Close," *Saginaw News* (December 3, 2005). http://www.mlive.com/hockey/sanews/index.ssf?/base/sports-0/1133608824299390.xml&coll=9.

Resource Guide

Consider this resource section as a way to continue your education. I've included books, articles, and films about many aspects of hazing in schools, colleges, and the military. In addition, I've suggested other kinds of books that are relevant for parents, teachers, coaches, and students.

These resources can be used in many ways. Some of the films depict common situations where hazing occurs, allowing a parent or teacher to discuss the conditions that encourage hazing. Other films graphically show hazing in action and the consequences of hazardous hazing. These films are often used in hazing awareness programs. Any of the books and articles could be required reading for health classes, for social science courses, and for new membership education training.

I hope these resources increase your knowledge of hazing so that you're well equipped to be an agent of change. The more you know about hazing, the more powerful you can be in educating others about hazing.

HAZING

Books

Be My Sorority Sister: Under Pressure, by Dorrie Williams-Wheeler. A
   pro-sorority novel seen through the eyes of young black women in

college. It includes many examples of hazing rituals and initiation practices. This easy-to-read book can be used to examine how sorority members think of and view their initiation rites.

Bleachers, by John Grisham. This quick-read novel allows you to experience the importance of small-town high school football in rural America. It focuses on the coach and his influence on the individuals and the team. This book can be used to discuss the role of authority figures and how they influence the team's behavior.

Black Haze: Violence, Sacrifice, and Manhood in Black Greek-Letter Fraternities, by Ricky L. Jones. This book provides an excellent analysis of hazing among black college students. Jones analyzes hazing rituals in five major black fraternities and examines how the violent hazing practices are important to the members' sense of self. This book could be used in academic settings in which it's important to understand masculinity and power and how they relate to hazing.

Goat: A Memoir, by Brad Land. Land's short, easy-to-read memoir of his fraternity pledge hazing is very powerful and realistic. It can be used with high school and college students to explore expectations of group membership, bonding, and issues about pledging and de-pledging.

High School Hazing: When Rites Become Wrongs, by Hank Nuwer. This is the first book to shine a light on hazing in high school, and it is a great primer on hazing issues in high school, in college, and in gangs. This book can be used as a way to discuss various aspects of hazing, including the role of alcohol.

Pledged: The Secret Life of Sororities, by Alexandra Robbins. The graphic descriptions of sorority life, including many kinds of hazing events, make this compelling book a must-read for those needing to know more about what drives women to join sororities. It provides ample material to begin discussions among high school and college students.

The Hazing Reader, edited by Hank Nuwer. Professionals from various disciplines share their beliefs about how hazing begins, why it continues, and how it can end.

Too Far, by Mike Lupica. This well-written novel explores the dynamics of high school hazing. It is appropriate for parents, teachers, coaches, and students. It's a great vehicle for opening discussions on the code of silence.

Wrongs of Passage: Fraternities, Sororities, Hazing and Binge Drinking, by Hank Nuwer. This book explores the history of hazing in exquisite detail. It also provides descriptions and examples of hazing and alcohol abuse on college campuses. This book is necessary for those building a library on hazing.

Web Sites

Alfred University Study. www.alfred.edu/hs_hazing. The Alfred University Study was the first major academic initiative on hazing. This Web site summarizes the hazing surveys completed in 1999 and 2000. The statistics provided are the ones used most frequently by newspapers, magazines, and television.

Campuspeak. www.campusspeak.com/cap/anti-hazing. This organization began National Hazing Prevention Week. It provides anti-hazing programs, including educational speakers, for college students.

Child Abuse Prevention Services (CAPS). www.kidsafe-caps.org. CAPS is a nonprofit organization that provides information on child abuse prevention, bullying, and hazing. Reports of child abuse and hazing can be made on this site.

Cornell University's Hazing Awareness Site. www.hazing.cornell.edu. This site is an excellent resource on many aspects of hazing in college. Cornell's Web site should be a model for other universities. It provides examples of hazing on the Cornell campus, as well as information on what to do if a student is being hazed.

Douglas Fierberg, Attorney. www.hazinglaw.com. Douglas Fierberg is the nation's leading expert on hazing law. This Web site provides information on Fierberg and other hazing resources.

Education Center for Alcohol and Other Drug Prevention. www.edc.org/hec/violence/hazing.html. This site is an important resource for alcohol education and for articles on hazing.

Hank Nuwer. http://hazing.hanknuwer.com. Hank Nuwer provides an immense wealth of important hazing information. He delineates high school and college hazings and provides a listing of reported hazings that have occurred since 1905.

Initiation Rites and Athletics for NCAA Sports Teams.
www.alfred.edu/sports_hazing/introduction.html. This is the
national study on hazing conducted by the NCAA and Alfred University. The statistics and findings from this important study are
often quoted in the media.

Inside Hazing. www.insidehazing.com. This is my Web site. It's designed
to explore the psychology of hazing. Simple answers to frequently
asked questions about hazing are given in a pragmatic way. Hazing
articles and current news events are included and updated frequently. There is also an online survey and methods to communicate with me directly.

KidsHealth. http://www.kidshealth.org. This site provides easy-to-read
information for parents and children about hazing, as well as other
health-related issues.

Mothers Against School Hazing (MASH). www.mashinc.org. Mothers
Against School Hazing was started by Karen Savoy after her son
was a victim of high school hazing. Karen shares her story and cor-
responds with parents and students who have their own story to
tell. MASH accepts reports of new hazing incidents and provides
guidance on the next steps to take. In addition, this Web site provides the hazing laws for every state.

National Hazing Prevention Week. www.nhpw.com. Campuspeak spon-
sors this site. It includes interviews and information on the annual
hazing prevention week, which occurs at the end of September.

Report-it. www.report-it.com. This unique service provides 24-hour,
365-day-a-year online reporting of any dangerous activity. Reports
can be made with full disclosure or anonymously. This site is a
great asset for school districts, universities, and other organizations
and should be a cornerstone for anti-hazing programs.

Security on Campus. www.securityoncampus.org/. This watchdog group
was created by the parents of a college student who was killed on
campus. The site specializes in violence prevention on college
campuses. It's been created to help parents evaluate colleges before
they send their child to the campus.

Sports Leadership Institute. www.adelphi.edu/communityservices/sli/.
Don McPherson, a former NFL player, created this site to improve

leadership in sports. The institute provides training programs for
coaches and athletes.

Stop Hazing.org. www.stophazing.org. Dr. Elizabeth Allen, a hazing
researcher, created this Web site to be a clearinghouse of useful
information on hazing. It provides links to current hazing news
and research, message boards on hazing related topics, and the hazing laws for every state.

The Gordie Foundation. http://www.gordie.org. The parents of Gordie
Bailey created this site to remember Gordie, a freshman who died
in a fraternity hazing, and to provide information about alcohol
and hazing.

We Miss You Matt. www.wemissyoumatt.com. The parents of Matt Carrington created this site to remember their son, a student who died
in a fraternity hazing. The site provides information about hazing
legislation in California.

Articles

Athletes Abusing Athletes. www.espn.go.com/otl/hazing/monday.html.
Part of ESPN's Web site, this series of articles reviews athletic hazing incidents in high school and college.

A Fraternity Hazing Gone Wrong. www.npr.org/templates/story/story.
php?storyId=5012154. Both an article and an audio interview
with Hank Nuwer about Matt Carrington, a pledge who died of
water intoxication during a fraternity hazing in February 2005.

*Brutal Rituals, Dangerous Rites: High School Hazing Grows Violent
and Humiliating*. http://www.asbj.com/2000/08/0800coverstory.
html. This article provides a good description of hazing in high
schools.

Greek Tragedy. http://www.deltasigmatheta.com/haze17.htm.
Greek Tragedy tells a story about hazing among black college
students.

Hazing: What's the Harm? http://www.americancatholic.org/Newsletters/
YU/ay0701.asp. An enlightening article for students that's supported by the Catholic Church.

Report on Hazing at UVM. http://universitycommunications.uvm.
edu/?Page=committee.htm. This site provides the actual report on

hazing developed by the University of Vermont in response to a
serious hazing event on their hockey team in 2000.

The Military's Hazing Hell. www.salon.com/mwt/feature/2004/06/04/
carol_burke/. Carol Burke, author of *Camp All-American, Hanoi
Jane and the High and Tight,* reports on hazing in the military.

The Sordid Side of Sports. http://www.usnews.com/usnews/edu/
articles/000911/archive_012912.htm. This *U.S. News and
World Report* article reviews many hazing incidents in high school
and college.

Films

Unless otherwise noted, all of these films can be purchased on Amazon.com.

A Few Good Men. This star-studded military courtroom drama is an
excellent film and will appeal to students and administrators alike.
Tom Cruise and Jack Nicholson deal with a murder, a hazing, and
most important, the code of silence. Significant issues to discuss
include the role of administrators in hazing and the implied message
that hazing is OK to teach a lesson.

Animal House. A classic comedy about college life and hazing may
seem to be the antithesis of what hazing activists want to encourage.
However, this lighthearted film can be a non-
threatening approach to opening up the topic of college life
and hazing.

Annapolis. This 2006 film, set in Annapolis, depicts military school life,
including hazing. *Annapolis* will provoke intense discussion on
whether hazing is a necessary part of military training.

Dazed and Confused. Much like *Animal House,* this humorous tale of
hazing in high school is a good place to start when discussing how
hazing begins and how it skids into the hazardous zone. It's particularly
relevant for high school students.

Drumline. This is a rare look at university marching bands. The story
highlights the needs of the individual versus the needs of the
group and can be used by non-athletic, non-Greek groups to open
discussions on hazing.

Frat House. Originally created for HBO and screened at the Sundance Film Festival, this film depicts college fraternity hazing. Many students will find scenes that are familiar and that resonate with their point of view. It's available at www.netflix.com.

Friday Night Lights. This film depicts high school football in the south and shows how very important the sport is to athletes, their parents, and the community. This film can be used as an easy introduction to the culture of sports and the role that parents play.

G.I. Jane. This twist on the typical military film stars Demi Moore, who proves that women can succeed as Navy Seals. However, before she is accepted by her peers, she is thoroughly "tested," in ways that look and feel like a hazing. It makes good material for examining the concept of *proving one's worthiness*.

Hamster Cocktails and the Truth About Hazing. The old adage "reality is stranger than fiction" is demonstrated in this short film, which shows college students throwing live hamsters into a blender as they create drinks for new pledges. This will begin a good discussion on the kinds of activities that students engage in and how and why such events occur. It's available at www.securityoncampus.org/videos.html.

Hoosiers. Gene Hackman stars as a coach of an underdog high school basketball team in Indiana. The film highlights what basketball means to the community, and the importance of the role of a coach. This is a great example of how a powerful coach can be a positive influence on the lives of his players and the community.

School Daze. Hazing in black fraternities and sororities had not been depicted in film until this Spike Lee movie. Among the many story lines in *School Daze*, a black college student wants to join a fraternity and is subjected to various hazing traditions. This film illustrates the fact that hazing occurs in all racial groups.

The Flight That Fought Back. This film is the Discovery Channel's reenactment of Flight 93, in which the passengers—themselves victims, bystanders, and heroes—changed the course of history on September 11, 2001. This is a great example of empowered bystanders working together. This is a surprisingly upbeat and emotional film that shows us all how we can be responsible individuals by working as a team. It's available at www. discovery.com.

The Lords of Discipline. Military hazing seems to be an accepted way of life for many. This film is set at the Carolina Military Institute, where a brutal hazing occurs. This film can be used with students and faculty in military high schools, in colleges, and in the military itself. It's available at www.barnesandnoble.com.

Training Day. This look into the LAPD has a star-studded cast, including Denzel Washington and Ethan Hawke. The film centers on the hazing of rookie policemen during a twenty-four-hour period. This movie will appeal to all audiences. It can be used to discuss how hazing is integrated and accepted in our society and the many ethical dilemmas we face because of it.

Unless a Death Occurred. This film was made by perpetrators, who reenacted the fraternity hazing of Walter Jennings, who died of water intoxication at SUNY Plattsburgh. It has been integrated into new-member education programs throughout the United States and demonstrates how hazing can skid into the hazardous zone. It's available at http://www.mountainlake.org/uado/uado.asp.

OTHER RESOURCES

Books for Parents

Building Moral Intelligence: The Seven Essential Virtues That Teach Kids to Do the Right Thing, by Michele Borba. Michele Borba gives insight into the concept of *moral intelligence* in our children, a necessary ingredient for a civilized society.

Queen Bees and Wannabes: Helping Your Daughter Survive Cliques, Gossip, Boyfriends, and Other Realities of Adolescence, by Rosalind Wiseman. Parents, teachers, and preadolescent girls will find this book a stimulating explanation of the hierarchy observed among teen girls.

Real Boys' Voices, by William Pollack. Listening to the inner feelings of boys aged ten to twenty will help readers understand the pressures that males face as they mature from boys to men.

*Staying Connected to Your Teenager: How to Keep Them Talking to You and
How to Hear What They're Really Saying,* by Michael Riera. This
book for parents portrays the adolescents' viewpoint and explains
their developmental needs.

*Understanding Teenage Depression: A Guide to Diagnosis, Treatment and
Management,* by Maureen Empfield and Nicholas Bakalar. This is a
parent's guide to recognizing and understanding why teens become
depressed, how they express it, and what you can do to help.

*Your Adolescent: Emotional, Behavioral, and Cognitive Development from
Early Adolescence Through the Teen Years,* by David Pruitt. A
pragmatic guide for parents, teachers, and counselors about common issues that face adolescents.

Books for Teachers

Holler If You Hear Me: The Education of a Teacher and His Students, by
Gregory Michie. A realistic and inspirational view of students and
teachers in middle and high school.

*Preparing Teachers for a Changing World: What Teachers Should Learn and
Be Able to Do,* by Linda Darling-Hammond and John Bransford.
This book targets those who train teachers and those who believe
that teachers should be prepared to equip their students with skills
for an evolving environment.

The Students Are Watching: Schools and the Moral Contract, by
Theodore R. Sizer and Nancy Faust Sizer. *The Students Are
Watching* strengthens the conviction that students do what we
do, not what we say. It empowers teachers to realize that they
are significant role models.

What Every Middle School Teacher Should Know, by Trudy Knowles
and Dave F. Brown. This easy-to-read book offers practical
and helpful information regarding preadolescent students and
their needs.

Books for Coaches

*Catch Them Being Good: Everything You Need to Know to Successfully
Coach Girls,* by Tony Dicicco. *Catch Them Being Good* contains
psychologically oriented tips on coaching girls.

Coach Carter, by Jasmine Jones. This engaging novel, inspired by true events, examines the power of a coach to positively affect the lives of his players.

Little League Drills and Strategies: Imaginative Practice Drills to Improve Skills and Attitude, by Ned McIntosh and Rich Cropper. This excellent resource for new and seasoned coaches on the many baseball fundamentals and drills also offers helpful suggestions on how to be a good coach, keep the game fun, and deal with overbearing parents and fans.

Positive Coaching: Building Character and Self-Esteem Through Sports, by Jim Thompson. *Positive Coaching* is chock full of stories and ideas to motivate and inspire.

Books for Adolescents

Chicken Soup for the Teenage Soul: Volumes One Through Four, by Jack Canfield, Mark Victor Hansen, Kimberly Kirberger, and Mitch Claspy. These easy-to-read anecdotes support adolescents in their struggles with identity, family, and friends.

Fighting Invisible Tigers: A Stress Management Guide for Teens, by Earl Hipp. This stress relief manual will help teens and those working with teens to reduce stress and relax. A matching workbook is also available.

Life Strategies for Teens, by Jay McGraw. Dr. Phil's son gives easy-to-read advice to teens. He challenges teens to take control of their lives and to become active and positive.

Reviving Ophelia: Saving the Selves of Adolescent Girls, by Mary Pipher. This book provides adolescent girls and their parents strategies to understand and protect against some of the typical dilemmas of teen culture.

The 7 Habits of Highly Effective Teens, by Sean Covey. Teens will find this a helpful road map for surviving adolescence and entering adulthood with strength and insight.

Books on Bullying

Bullying Prevention Handbook: A Guide for Principals, Teachers, and Counselors, by John H. Hoover and Ronald Oliver. This is a good teaching tool for incorporating anti-bullying lessons in school.

Push & Shove, by Jim Boulden. *Push & Shove* was written for young students, so they could experience life through the eyes of the bully and the victim.

Stick Up for Yourself: Every Kid's Guide to Personal Power and Positive Self-Esteem, by Gershen Kaufman, Lev Raphael, and Pamela Espel. This book provides kids with methods they can use to stop being victimized.

The Bully, the Bullied, and the Bystander, from Preschool to High School: How Parents and Teachers Can Help Break the Cycle of Violence, by Barbara Coloroso. Coloroso's book is an excellent, wide-angle view of bullying and how to stop it.

The Parent's Guide to Protecting Your Children in Cyberspace, by Parry Aftab. This book offers advice for parents about dealing with online bullying.

About the Author

Susan Lipkins, Ph.D., a psychologist for over twenty years, maintains a private practice, where she specializes in children and adolescents. She began her career in anthropology, completing an independent study with Dr. Margaret Mead. On her way to a doctorate and post-doctorate work in psychology, Lipkins received a master's degree in special education and early childhood education. She has also been a college professor and school psychologist.

Lipkins has researched and interviewed those who haze and have been hazed. She has conducted surveys and workshops and has analyzed the many facets of hazing. She has produced *Betrayal*, a documentary on hazing. Dr. Lipkins answers the important questions about the psychology of hazing. She illustrates why hazing survives, how it is transmitted, and what you can do to stop it.

She has appeared on NBC's *Today Show* and the YES Network, as well as on radio stations throughout the United States. In addition, she has been quoted and published in the *Wall Street Journal*, the *New York Times*, the *New York Post*, the *New York Daily News*, and numerous newspapers and Internet sites throughout the world. She has presented her research at the American Psychological Association's annual convention.

Dr. Lipkins invites readers to learn more about hazing at her Web site, www.insidehazing.com.

Index